TOBIAS SMOLLETT

Modern Critical Views

These and other titles in preparation

Modern Critical Views

TOBIAS SMOLLETT

Edited and with an introduction by
Harold Bloom
Sterling Professor of the Humanities
Yale University

83272

CHELSEA HOUSE PUBLISHERS ◇ 1987
New York ◇ New Haven ◇ Philadelphia

Library of Congress Cataloging-in-Publication Data
Tobias Smollett.
   (Modern critical views)
   Bibliography: p.
   Includes index.
   Summary: A collection of critical essays on Smollet
and his works arranged in chronological order of
publication.
   1. Smollett, Tobias George, 1721–1771—Criticism and
interpretation. [1. Smollet, Tobias George, 1721–1771—
Criticism and interpretation. 2. English literature—
History and criticism] I. Bloom, Harold. II. Series.
PR3697.T596   1987   823'.6   87–5182
ISBN 1–55546–282–0 (alk. paper)

Contents

Editor's Note

This book brings together a representative selection of the best modern criticism devoted to the novels of Tobias Smollett. The critical essays are reprinted here in the chronological order of their original publication. I am grateful to Christina Büchmann for her erudition and judgment in helping me to edit this volume.

My introduction is an appreciation of *Humphry Clinker,* examining the paradox of Smollett's quest for health, sanity, and proportion in a fictive world that he declines to endow with those qualities, and with fictive characters who tend to eccentricity, roughness, and an antipathetic grotesquerie. Ronald Paulson begins the chronological sequence of criticism with an overview of the alternation of melodramatic satire and sentimental idealization in Smollett's novels, an alternation that Paulson sees "successfully embodied in Bramble," the hero of *Humphry Clinker.*

In a study of the grotesque in *Humphry Clinker,* Robert Hopkins judges its function, particularly in Bramble's earlier vision of reality, as being precisely parallel to the function of irony in Swift and in Fielding, a subversive gesture made against a diseased society. T. O. Treadwell, considering *Ferdinand Count Fathom,* concludes that it succeeds as a bitter comedy satirizing a monstrous seducer and confidence man. Surveying the mode of the picaresque in Smollett, Philip Stevick evaluates only *Humphry Clinker* as bringing into balance a need for joyous play and an equal need for a harmony of existence, a balance clearly not achieved in *Peregrine Pickle* or *Roderick Random.* Thomas R. Preston analyzes Smollett's characterization in terms of the influence of the "stage passions" of eighteenth-century theater, while Michael Rosenblum traces the role of romance conventions in Smollett's fantasy-laden father-son reunions. Smollett's curiously mixed mode of representation is seen by Paul-Gabriel Boucé as a comic realism that avoids a dead-level reductionism.

The style of Smollett is studied by Damian Grant as a precise mode of comic mischief-making, after which this book concludes with Jerry C. Beasley's comparison of Smollett to Richardson and Fielding as transformers of private experience into public history.

Introduction

Despite the vigor and humor of *Humphry Clinker,* Smollett is currently the most neglected of the major eighteenth-century British novelists. Since he is not of the aesthetic eminence of Richardson, Fielding, and Sterne, one would not expect him to provoke the intense critical interest that they perpetually sustain. But *Humphry Clinker,* in my judgment, is a stronger novel than Defoe's *Moll Flanders* or Goldsmith's *The Vicar of Wakefield,* and compares favorably also with Fanny Burney's *Evelina.* Since it is now less read and studied than any of those three, its eclipse perhaps indicates that something in Smollett is not available to what is dominant in our current sensibility. The era of Thomas Pynchon, apocalyptic and beyond the resources of any satiric vision, is not a time for accommodating Smollett's rough tumble of an expedition towards a yearned-for health.

Smollett, a surgeon, probably knew he had not long to live even as he composed *Humphry Clinker.* Resident in Italy from 1768 on, for his health, Smollett died there in 1771, just fifty, some three months after *Humphry Clinker* was published. The expedition that is the novel, winding from Wales up through the length of England well into Smollett's native Scotland, is the author's long farewell to life, rendering Britain with a peculiar vividness as he remembers it from abroad.

Why the novel is named for Humphry Clinker rather than its central figure, Matthew Bramble, who clearly is Smollett's surrogate, never has been clear to me, except that Clinker is a representative of the future and may be Smollett's wistful introjection of a life he would not survive to know. Clinker and Bramble rise together from the water, a natural son and the father he has saved from drowning, and both undergo a change of name into the same name: Matthew Loyd. This curious mutual baptism seems to have been a mythic transference for Smollett, since Matthew Loyd was Bramble's *former* name, and will be his son Humphry Clinker's *future* name. It is as though the slowly dying Smollett required a double

1

vision of survival: as a Matthew Bramble largely purged of an irascibility close to madness, and as Humphry Clinker, a kindly and innocent youth restored to a lost heritage.

I have found that many of my friends and students, generally very good readers, shy away from *Humphry Clinker* and from Smollett in general, because they are repelled by his mode, which at its strongest tends toward grotesque farce. The mode by definition is not pleasant, but, like the much greater Swift, Smollett is a master in this peculiar subgenre. It is hardly accidental that Thomas Rowlandson illustrated Smollett in the early 1790s, because there is a profound affinity between the novelist and the caricaturist. Smollett's reality, at its most intense, is phantasmagoric, and there are moments early on in *Humphry Clinker* when the irritable (and well-named) Bramble seems close to madness. His speculations on the origins of the waters at Bath are not less than disgusting, and he is more than weary of mankind: "My curiosity is quite satisfied: I have done with the science of men, and must now endeavour to amuse myself with the novelty of things." Everywhere he finds only "food for spleen, and subject for ridicule."

Bramble satirizes everything he encounters, and is himself an instance of the mocker mocked or the satirist satirized. One can cultivate an amused affection for him, but he is not Don Quixote, and the vivid but unlikable Lismahago, my favorite character in the book, is no Sancho Panza. Smollett evidently identifies with Bramble, but we cannot do so, and surely Smollett intended it that way. We may enjoy farce, but we do not wish to find ourselves acting in one as we stumble on in our lives. I think of my favorite farce in the language, Marlowe's *The Jew of Malta*. I have acted on stage just once in my life, playing Falstaff in an emergency, an amateur pressed into service, and played the witty knight more or less in the style of the late, great Zero Mostel playing Leopold Bloom in *Ulysses in Nighttown*. The one part I would love to play on stage is Barabas, bloody Jew of Malta, but in life obviously I would prefer being Falstaff to being Barabas.

When a novel conducts itself as realistic farce, which is Smollett's mode, we are denied the pleasures of introjection and identification. But a novel is wiser to forsake realism when it moves into farce. Sometimes I wish, reading Smollett, that he had been able to read the Evelyn Waugh of *Decline and Fall, Vile Bodies, A Handful of Dust,* because I think that Waugh would have been a good influence upon him. But that is to wish Smollett other than Smollett; one of his strengths is that he drives realistic representation almost beyond its proper limits, in order to extend the empire of farce. Perhaps his own fierce temperament required the extension, for he was more than a little mad, in this resembling certain elements of temperament in Swift, Sterne, and Dr. Samuel Johnson.

Sterne, in *A Sentimental Journey,* robustly satirizes Smollett as "the learned Smelfungus", who "set out with the spleen and jaundice, and every object he passed by was discoloured or distorted." Coming out of the Pantheon, Smelfungus comments, " 'Tis nothing but a huge cock pit," and all his travel adventures lead to similar judgments, provoking Sterne to a good retort: "I'll tell it, cried Smelfungus, to the world. You had better tell it, said I, to your physician." All of us would rather travel with Sterne than with Smollett, but reading Smollett remains a uniquely valuable experience. Let us take him at his most ferociously grotesque, in the account of the sufferings of Lismahago and the still more unfortunate Murphy at the horrid hands of the Miami Indians:

> By dint of her interrogations, however, we learned, that he and ensign Murphy had made their escape from the French hospital at Montreal, and taken to the woods, in hope of reaching some English settlement; but mistaking their route, they fell in with a party of Miamis, who carried them away in captivity. The intention of these Indians was to give one of them as an adopted son to a venerable sachem, who had lost his own in the course of the war, and to sacrifice the other according to the custom of the country. Murphy, as being the younger and handsomer of the two, was designed to fill the place of the deceased, not only as the son of the sachem, but as the spouse of a beautiful squaw, to whom his predecessor had been betrothed; but in passing through the different whigwhams or villages of the Miamis, poor Murphy was so mangled by the women and children, who have the privilege of torturing all prisoners in their passage, that, by the time they arrived at the place of the sachem's residence, he was rendered altogether unfit for the purposes of marriage: it was determined therefore, in the assembly of the warriors, that ensign Murphy should be brought to the stake, and that the lady should be given to lieutenant Lismahago, who had likewise received his share of torments, though they had not produced emasculation.—A joint of one finger had been cut, or rather sawed off with a rusty knife; one of his great toes was crushed into a mash betwixt two stones; some of his teeth were drawn, or dug out with a crooked nail;

splintered reeds had been thrust up his nostrils and other tender parts; and the calves of his legs had been blown up with mines of gunpowder dug in the flesh with the sharp point of the tomahawk.

The Indians themselves allowed that Murphy died with great heroism, singing, as his death song, the *Drimmendoo,* in concert with Mr. Lismahago, who was present at the solemnity. After the warriors and the matrons had made a hearty meal upon the muscular flesh which they pared from the victim, and had applied a great variety of tortures, which he bore without flinching, an old lady, with a sharp knife, scooped out one of his eyes, and put a burning coal in the socket. The pain of this operation was so exquisite that he could not help bellowing, upon which the audience raised a shout of exultation, and one of the warriors stealing behind him, gave him the *coup de grace* with a hatchet.

Lismahago's bride, the squaw Squinkinacoosta, distinguished herself on this occasion.—She shewed a great superiority of genius in the tortures which she contrived and executed with her own hands.—She vied with the stoutest warrior in eating the flesh of the sacrifice; and after all the other females were fuddled with dram-drinking, she was not so intoxicated but that she was able to play the game of the platter with the conjuring sachem, and afterwards go through the ceremony of her own wedding, which was consummated that same evening. The captain had lived very happily with this accomplished squaw for two years, during which she bore him a son, who is now the representative of his mother's tribe; but, at length, to his unspeakable grief, she had died of a fever, occasioned by eating too much raw bear, which they had killed in a hunting excursion.

This is both dreadfully funny and funnily dreadful, and is quite marvelous writing, though evidently not to all tastes. If it were written by Mark Twain, we would know how to take it, but Smollett renders it with a dangerous relish, which makes us a little uncertain, since we do not wish to be quite as rancid as the learned Smelfungus, or even as the dreadful Lismahago for that matter. Reading Smollett is sometimes like eating too much raw bear, but that only acknowledges how authentic and strong his flavor is.

To have inspired Rowlandson and fostered Charles Dickens (who took his origins in a blend of Smollett and Ben Jonson) is enough merit for any one writer. Smollett is to Dickens what Marlowe was to Shakespeare, a forerunner so swallowed up by an enormous inheritor that the precursor sometimes seems a minnow devoured by a whale. But, considered in himself, Smollett has something of Marlowe's eminence. Each carried satirical farce and subversive melodrama to a new limit, and that too is merit enough.

·RONALD PAULSON

Satire and Melodrama

In *Roderick Random* Smollett connects evil with the effects of egotism—the impingement of one individual upon the liberty, security, or serenity of another. He associates this with the authority of captains and generals, the rich and politically powerful. But in *Peregrine Pickle*, by which time *Clarissa* had been published, his emphasis changes from the public types of dominance to the private and, increasingly, the sexual. He shows the desire for power over other people in satirists, wives, and seducers; the first part of the novel is about marriage, the second about extramarital relations, and in both the unit of analysis is the relationship between a man and a woman.

The first volume gives various examples of subjection and freedom in a comic context. Two men appear at the outset, one completely passive, already dominated by his sister, and the other free. Gamaliel Pickle merely exchanges one keeper for another when he marries; but Hawser Trunnion is captured and subdued, his eccentricity curbed, by a wife. What at first seems their folly soon turns out to be innocence. In the society of these women they are "quite out of their element"; they have no chance against the "discretion," prudence, and scheming of the single-minded Grizzle and the new Mrs. Pickle. Smollett contrasts a preternatural simplicity with a dedication to deceit and domination. With Grizzle in charge of the Trunnion ménage, "in less than two hours, the whole economy of the garrison was turned topsy-turvy" (chap. 9); "in less than three months he became

From *Satire and the Novel in Eighteenth-Century England.* © 1967 by Yale University. Yale University Press, 1967.

7

a thorough-paced husband" (chap. 10). Throughout the story poor Trunnion is compared with captive animals; "like a reluctant bear, . . . he is led to the stake amidst the shouts and cries of butchers and their dogs" (chap. 5).

The story of Pickle and Trunnion in the first volume is a parallel and preparation for the whole story of Peregrine, with special emphasis on his heredity. But a significant change takes place as Smollett's focus narrows from the contrasted Trunnion and Pickle households to the story of Peregrine himself. The various kinds of exploitation narrow to a preoccupation with a single kind, sexual violation, and the various innocences of Trunnion and Pickle become the single, and supposedly far more important, innocence of the helpless virgin. Although the attempt to rape Emilia is not the exclusive consequence of Peregrine's will to power, Smollett seems to regard it as his climactic and most heinous crime, which must be elaborately expiated. Peregrine approaches the rape via the beating of Pallet and the ducking of Hornbeak, via the seduction of one wife and the attempted seduction of another. The worst is his nearly successful rape of a virgin. Such scenes of more-or-less bungled seduction are a commonplace of *Gil Blas* and the continental picaresque, but here the tone of moral concern or indignation is much stronger; the reader feels that Peregrine is doing something evil as well as foolish, and not that this is simply the way of the world. The style reflects the situation:

> Instead of awful veneration, which her presence used to inspire, that chastity of sentiment, and delicacy of expression, he now gazed upon her with the eyes of a libertine, he glowed with the impatience of desire, talked in a strain that barely kept within the bounds of decency.

Although Peregrine's attempt to rape Emilia is motivated by his pride and (Smollett adds for good measure) his adherence to the false ideals of high society, the heightened feeling Smollett engenders around the act derives almost exclusively from the idea of Peregrine's forcibly deflowering the girl who loves him and (the irony of his self-delusion) whom he loves. One of Smollett's direct sources is Mrs. Davys's *Accomplish'd Rake* (1727), and the difference is instructive. He omits the large quotient of Sir John Galliard's obligations to the Friendly family and the elaborate consequences to them as well as to the raped Miss Friendly; the horror of the unaccomplished rape in *Peregrine Pickle* is made to arise more exclusively from the sexual situation.

In *Ferdinand Count Fathom* the seduction/rape becomes Smollett's chief symbol of evil (the robbery is a less heinous analogue), and his ap-

proach to sexual evil is less equivocal, perhaps because he now has an almost completely unsympathetic hero. Fathom's schemes and attempts at
sexual violation mark his progress toward an absolute in depravity. The
five seductions (or attempted seductions) are a major unifying element in
the novel and appear increasingly worse as the women attacked are progressively more innocent.

Teresa, the first victim, is merely an unscrupulous servant, no better
than Fathom, who helps him cheat the Melvils. The second victim, Wilhelmina, is an unattractive girl who succumbs to gross flattery, and her
stepmother, who receives the same treatment, is played off against her.
Wilhelmina has such clearly designated weaknesses of character as "unen-
lightened pride" and (with her stepmother) a certain "appetite for pleasure" (chap. 12). The reader is told in passing that Fathom debauches the
landlord's daughter in Antwerp and leaves her four months pregnant
(chap. 27), but there are no details given. The next victim, Elenor, is a
more complex and pathetic case. Fathom meets her on the stage to London
and quickly convinces her that she has "captivated the heart of a man who
could raise her to the rank and dignity of a countess." She is essentially
"an innocent, unsuspecting country damsel, flushed with the warmth of
youth, and an utter stranger to the ways of life" (chap. 30), and her fate
is accordingly darker than Wilhelmina's. Celinda, as we have seen, is motivated by excessive sensibility, but her consequences are the most dismay-
ing, a plunge from degradation to degradation. Significantly, Mlle. de Melvil and Monimia, who have none of these follies, do not follow the path
to seduction. With them, as with Emilia, the seducer cannot succeed, and
Smollett has settled into the world of melodrama in which villains are
thwarted and heroines preserved.

Smollett informs this scene of sexual threat with the vocabulary of
melodrama and its appurtenances of tears, religious overtones, and physical fear. The diction heightens three areas—the evil seducer, the pursued
innocent, and the atmosphere that surrounds the act of evil. Peregrine is
"the insidious lover" who works upon Emilia with "his hypocrisy" until
"her heart should be so far entangled within his snares" that he can seduce
her (chap. 75). Fathom "marks" Elenor's "chastity for prey to his volup-
tuous passion" (chap. 30). On the supposed death of Monimia, the narrator addresses Fathom thus: "Perfidious wretch! thy crimes turn out to be
so atrocious, that I half repent me of having undertaken to record thy
memoirs; yet such monsters ought to be exhibited to public view" (chap.
49). This is still clearly the Juvenalian world in which Swift flays Lord Al-
len and puts his carcass on display, but the satiric grotesque is becoming
monstrous, sublimely horrible. Juvenal's wives who poison their husbands

and the sons who poison their fathers are only somewhat more grotesque and less melodramatic.

Another extension of the Juvenalian situation is the pitiful victim—the Umbricius who is driven out of Rome. When Fathom tells Monimia his lies about her beloved Renaldo, "her fatal conjecture" about Renaldo's love brings out "signs of extreme agitation"; "a flood of tears gushed from her enchanting eyes"; "she indulged her sorrow to excess" (chap. 45). She "endeavoured to devour her griefs in silence; she in secret bemoaned her forlorn fate without ceasing; her tears flowed without intermission from night to morn, and from morn to night" (chap. 46). And so "her cheeks grew wan, her bright eyes lost their splendour, the roses vanished from her lips, and her delicate limbs could hardly support their burden." As Fathom moves in for the kill, she resists his "detested embrace," and the resulting clash is almost "supernatural" (to use Smollett's word): he "would have acted the part of young Tarquin, and violated by force that sacred shrine of honour, beauty, and unblemished truth" (chap. 49). She, with sword in hand, is like the archangel Michael; her aspect "seemed to shine with something supernatural, and actually disordered his whole faculties"—and he, like Satan, retreats.

The virgin is only the extreme instance of innocence and pitiableness. The reaction of Monimia's beloved Renaldo to Fathom's plot is much the same: separated from Monimia his life becomes "a sacrifice to the most poignant distress"; "he beheld the mistress of his soul abandoned to the blackest scenes of poverty and want" (chap. 44); and he too "wept and raved by turns" (chap. 46). As Smollett tells the reader in a chapter heading, "Renaldo's Distress Deepens, and Fathom's Plot thickens" (chap. 45). Much as Fielding does in *Jonathan Wild*, Smollett shows a thesis, Fathom, and an antithesis, Renaldo Melvil: the first volume is about Fathom, the second increasingly about Melvil—in particular about the reactions of the innocent as they are exploited by the evil Fathom, and so about their suffering. The focus on Melvil and his particular suffering at Fathom's hands shows how, by shifting to the victim, Smollett has changed from the comic or grotesque to a melodramatic evil, from the vigor of evil to the agonies of the persecuted innocent, and from indignation to compassion.

In such surroundings evil becomes palpable, an atmosphere, as in parts of *Macbeth*. The well-known interlude of Fathom's seeking refuge from a storm in a lonely house on the way to Paris introduces this atmosphere. The house in which guests are murdered for their money, the stormy night, the "dismal soughing of the trees," lightning and thunder and rain, and a murdered man still warm elicit from Fathom "unspeakable horror" and "transports of . . . dread" (chap. 21). Smollett's point in introducing this scene is presumably to warn Fathom (and the reader) of the depths to which he will sink—that murder for money is not far beyond murder for lust (which appears to be Monimia's fate). More important are the elements of the Gothic and the sublime which Smollett associates with the manifestation of evil—as he does later in the visit to Monimia's "grave" and in her "ghost" and "resurrection."

Smollett's introduction of such scenes and imagery is, in one sense, a matter of decorum. Critics increasingly warned satirists that evil and vice should not be ridiculed; ridicule was to be reserved for lighter follies. Moreover, ridicule remained a low form compared to the "finer perception" of the sense of sublimity which was supposedly beyond the satirist. One solution was Smollett's—to modulate from one tone to another or to show the close connections that existed between satire and Gothic horror and other aspects of the sublime.

Smollett's melodrama operates by the same externalizing of emotion and generalizing of diction that characterizes his satire. When terror comes to Commodore Trunnion, "a cold sweat bedewed his limbs, his knees knocked together, his hair bristled up, and the remains of his teeth were shattered to pieces in the convulsive vibrations of his jaws" (chap. 7). If Trunnion batters his teeth to pieces in comic terror, with Fathom "the whole surface of his body was covered with a cold sweat, and his nerves were relaxed with an universal palsy" (chap. 21). Rape and seduction are only the obverse of the satiric violence of broken heads and violent purges. Smollett's theory can be described either as the belief that satire and melodrama are complementary and can be mixed—that they are, after all, both heightenings of reality—or that such melodramatic episodes as the seduction scene are an extension and darkening of satire, much like the harsh railing style that the satirist assumes when the world becomes too incorrigible for any other approach.

There is satiric precedence for Smollett's linking satire with melodrama in parts of Juvenal's satires and in Elizabethan satire (especially in a work like Nashe's *Unfortunate Traveller*). But it is more probably from the novels of Mrs. Manley and Mrs. Haywood, which called themselves satires, that Smollett derived the plausible idea that scenes of raped innocence, sexual violence, and heavily emotional trappings could complement or intensify satire. The seduction of Celinda, for example, could have been written by Mrs. Manley; it leads to the familiar consequences, with the poor girl growing "every day more sensual and degenerate" and ending as a streetwalker. Her omniscient Cupid or Virtue or Justice may even have exerted some influence on Smollett's railing and—in *Fathom*—lamenting satirist and certainly on his omniscient atom in *Adventures of an Atom*.

Manley and Haywood, as well as Ward and Brown, offered another useful precedent to Smollett. If the satiric form can, under certain circumstances, absorb a series of melodramatic scenes, it can with equal ease be "intensified" into journalistic exposé. Again Juvenal offered an ultimate sanction in his lurid particularity, which could be interpreted as a *chronique scandaleuse* of Roman vice, but Mrs. Manley and the "secret histories" of the various "spies" were closer to hand. Smollett's narrative of Miss Williams's sad sexual experiences in *Roderick Random* is an early example of one aspect of the *chronique scandaleuse* (Melopoyne's story is another), but the most obvious is "The Memoirs of a Lady of Quality," which fills nearly a whole volume of *Peregrine Pickle* and deals with contemporary characters thinly disguised in a sentimental and sensational way, but with satiric touches. With Smollett, however, it is not altogether certain that his satire was not aiming toward some version of the actual, and that his long interval of composing histories and compendiums of knowledge was not in fact part of a straight line connecting *Roderick Random* and *Humphry Clinker*. Certainly one of the impressive accomplishments of the latter novel is its incorporation of journalistic elements.

Looking back from *Humphry Clinker*, we can see that exposé, the travel book, and the melodramatic and sentimental scenes are not only areas of subject matter but projected attitudes toward experience. In one sense all of the different tones—satiric (Horatian and Juvenalian), melodramatic, sentimental, reportorial—are attitudes, reflections of sensibility that resolve themselves into the general points of view of the letter writers in *Humphry Clinker*. However, they pose the central question of whether Smollett's use of them is, in intention and effect, the broadening of a spectrum or a transformation downward from Horatian satire to good-natured banter, from Juvenalian satire to melancholy, melodrama, and sublimity, and from admiration for the good to sentimental rapture? In one sense Smollett is consciously attempting to extend the satiric tone from indignation to horror and sympathy and the satiric subject matter from fool and knave to villain, from dupe to innocent virgin, from social to private, and from fancy to fact. This is, I think, the crucial intention, but one cannot discount the desire to write a popular work, because almost all the forms Smollett employs are popular contemporary ones—the *chronique*, the romance of rape and redemption, the journey about town (or country), and many more. In each case he borrows a form that has satiric roots but has lost most of its satiric inspiration. His motive was partly to revivify the satiric impulse but very likely partly to write popular fiction.

Peregrine Pickle was published in February 1751 and Fielding's *Amelia* in December of the same year (the dedication is dated December 12).

From what is known of Fielding's activities at the time, *Amelia* seems to have been written mainly in the course of that year. It is possible that Fielding read *Peregrine Pickle* upon publication, since the first edition contained scurrilous attacks on him and his friend Lyttelton; he alludes to the "Memoirs of a Lady of Quality" at least twice in the course of *Amelia*. Whatever the relationship between these novels, Amelia, the epitome of goodness, represents a remarkable reversal of her author's values. As the central symbol of value she is presented as the object of seducers, and the evil under consideration becomes the violation of sexual fidelity. Indeed Amelia is another Clarissa, whose problem is treated within the marriage relation, and who is ultimately successful in maintaining her integrity: she represents the "virtue rewarded" ending that Fielding claims to have wished Richardson would accord Clarissa. Mrs. Bennet's exclamation after the "fatal consequence" of the Noble Lord's attack on her virtue, "happy had I been had this been the period of my life" (bk. 7, chap. 7), exactly echoes Pamela's "May I never survive, one moment, that fatal one in which I shall forfeit my innocence!" While Mrs. Bennet does not escape Fielding's irony, in this instance her own sad fate is a warning to Amelia.

This is not to say that Fielding has suddenly adopted the Puritan ethic. Sexual intemperance in both *Tom Jones* and *Amelia* is a serious offense only when it injures someone, when it betrays Sophia or Amelia. It is not vague and irrational as in the works of Smollett. Moreover, Booth, driven by passion and seduced by Miss Matthews, is clearly less culpable than Colonel James, who is driven by passion to destroy his friend and an innocent woman; even worse are the Ellisons and Trents, who betray for pay, or the Noble Lord, who betrays for his own amusement. Nevertheless, in *Tom Jones* the sexual is only one of many kinds of violation; in *Amelia* it is the central one, with Booth's various misfortunes merely leading toward or away from the potential seduction of Amelia.

Fielding apparently felt that this aspect of *Amelia*, among others, needed some justification. Not long after *Amelia*'s publication he wrote some pieces about his "favourite child" in his current periodical, the *Covent-Garden Journal*. One of these essays (although not mentioning *Amelia* by name) discusses the idea of evil, those men "by whom [women] are deceived, corrupted, betrayed, and often brought *to Destruction, both Body and Soul*." The crime as he outlines it is appropriately Satanic—evil hating and wishing to destroy the good. In *Amelia* Satan, the Seducer of Man, becomes more specifically the Noble Lord, the Seducer of Women. He has all the Satanic trappings, whether satiric or Richardsonian. He is "the handsomest and genteelest person in the world" (bk. 7, chap. 6), a consummate actor, who carries out his seductions with masks; he corrupts his victims and then leaves them—corrupting is all that interests him. "What is this appetite," cries Mrs. Bennet, one of his victims, "which must have novelty and resistance for its provocatives, and which is delighted with us no longer than while we may be considered in the light of enemies?" (bk. 7, chap. 9). She has the last word on his crime:

> my doubt is whether the art or folly of it be the more conspicuous; for however delicate and refined the art must be allowed to have been, the folly, I think, must upon a fair examination appear no less astonishing: for to lay all considerations of cruelty and crime out of the case, what a foolish bargain doth the man make for himself who purchases so poor a pleasure at so high a price!
>
> (bk. 7, chap. 6)

By the last phrase she means both the enormous time and expense the Noble Lord went to in accomplishing his scheme and the price of his own soul. Fielding has once more put his villain in the Augustan context of Satan-Quixote.

As Fielding shows, the satirist could do one of two things. In his early work Fielding tried to establish some perspective on sexual evil, opposing the trivial evil of Pamela's situation to the real evil in ordinary social relationships. The other possibility was to accept the assumption of sexual evil; but since sexual evil was no laughing matter, the seduction would have to receive the overtones of Juvenalian indignation and melodramatic complaint.

Perhaps the most remarkable fact about both *Amelia* and the novels of Smollett, however, is their alternation of satiric and satiro-melodramatic scenes with visions of the good which are idealized and sentimentalized. A scene in Fielding's best satiric manner will be followed by a depiction of goodness painted in sharply contrasted colors. While Fielding leaves the reader to react to the satiric exposure, in the sentimental scenes he lets his characters do the reacting: Booth "stopped, and a torrent of tears gushed from his eyes—such tears as are apt to flow from a truly noble heart at the hearing of anything surprisingly great and glorious" (bk. 2, chap. 1). Virtuous behavior is also as stylized as the grotesque wambling of satiric characters: fearful for the safety of her son, Amelia "staggered toward him as fast as she could, all pale and breathless, and scarce able to support her tottering limbs" (bk. 4, chap. 7).

Although Smollett spends considerably less time than Fielding on the good characters, his villains tend to weep when confronted by the goodness they are in the process of destroying. Peregrine, when he attempts to ravish Emilia, finds "the tears gushing from his eyes" (chap. 76), which recalls his final attempt on Amanda, when "the tears ran down his cheeks" (chap. 58). Smollett, with his curious protagonists, is able to bring satire and sentimentality together in a single figure. Roderick's satiric railing is a symptom of a tendency to overreact to stimuli, which is also reflected in its opposite, pity, as when, finding Miss Williams in distress, he cries, "What effect, then, must it have had on [my heart] that was naturally prone to very tender passion?" A sentimentality that is the obverse of an extreme sensibility to evil or folly in its various disguises is best conveyed in Matthew Bramble, who, witnessing noble scenes like the return of Captain Brown, "sobbed, and wept, and clapt his hands, and hollowed" (Sept. 21). His nephew Jery explains that "His blood rises at every instance of insolence and cruelty. . . . On the other hand, the recital of a generous, humane, or grateful action, never fails to draw from him tears of approbation, which he is often greatly distressed to conceal" (May 10). Satire and sentiment, which appear rather unconvincingly side by side in Smollett's early and middle novels and in *Amelia*, are successfully embodied in Bramble as alternating reactions to experience.

If Smollett and Fielding demonstrate a willingness to see satire and various forms of sentimentality as complementary aspects of experience, it is not surprising to find a tradition of satire in the novel that carries this premise deep into the nineteenth century. Dickens is only the greatest example of the satiric logic we have examined carried to an extreme. The passage at the beginning of the fifth chapter of *Martin Chuzzlewit* (1843) sums up the distinctive quality of Dickens's satire (though not of course its most sterling qualities). The chapter begins with a brilliant satiric portrait of Pecksniff by describing his horse, in whom his enemies

> pretended to detect a fanciful resemblance to his master. Not in his outward person, for he was a rawboned, haggard horse, always on a much shorter allowance of corn than Mr. Pecksniff; but in his moral character, wherein, said they, he was full of promise, but of no performance. He was always, in a manner, going to go, and never going. When at his slowest rate of travelling, he would sometimes lift up his legs so high, and display such mighty action, that it was difficult to believe he was doing less than fourteen miles an hour; and he was for ever so perfectly satisfied with his own speed, and so little disconcerted by opportunities of comparing himself with the fastest trotters, that the illusion was the more difficult of resistance. He was a

kind of animal who infused into the breasts of strangers a lively
sense of hope, and possessed all those who knew him better
with a grim despair.

This portrait, in which the high and the low are both realized, is immediately followed by a passage describing the horse's driver:

> Blessings on thy simple heart, Tom Pinch, how proudly dost
> thou button up that scanty coat, called by a sad misnomer, for
> these many years, a "great" one. . . . Who, as thou drivest off,
> a happy man, and noddest with a grateful lovingness to Peck-
> sniff in his nightcap at his chamber-window, would not cry:
> "Heaven speed thee, Tom, and send that thou were going off
> for ever to some quiet home where thou mightest live at peace,
> and sorrow should not touch thee!"

The pairing of the satiric and grossly sentimental is a Dickens trademark.
The evil is fantastic in its symbolic vividness, and so is the good. If one
regards satire as a propagandistic device of persuasion which employs fantasy, irony, and other devices, he might well conclude that portraits of
both the good and the evil were called for in an equally "satiric" or fantastic tone. In Dickens's novels the satiric symbol like Pecksniff is comple-
mented, on the one hand, by the sentimental ideal he is grinding into the
ground, Tom Pinch, and, on the other, by the murderous and melodramatic Jonas Chuzzlewit. The rape of the innocent girl, the exploitation of
the child, and the murder of the rival all involve both a murderous exaggeration of a satiric vice (as Chuzzlewit is of Pecksniff) which is the center
of the novel, and an innocent virgin or orphan who is persecuted, but
brave and good.

The other extreme to which the satiric-sentimental dichotomy can
lead is a Gothic novel like Mrs. Radcliffe's *Mysteries of Udolpho* (1794),
where the emphasis is on the sentimental-melodramatic elements, which
are alternated (or padded) with satiric portraits and scenes. M. Quesnel,
Mme. Cheron, Count Morano, and others engage in situations in which
manners are juxtaposed and criticized and the innocent heroine is isolated
and persecuted. Once again the satiric and sentimental are related as different versions of a similar tone: the satiric scenes of tyranny with the Ques-
nels and Cherons work up to the "sublime" scenes at Montoni's Udolpho.
Although these characters have their prototypes in Clarissa's family, they
are observed satirically with Smollettian exaggeration; they are not real
people with complex motivations but, in their own way, obsessed souls
like Montoni.

ROBERT HOPKINS

The Function of Grotesque
in Humphry Clinker

We have yet to comprehend the full significance of the grotesque in Tobias Smollett's fiction. Although "grotesque" is frequently used in discussions of Smollett's achievement, one senses that until very recently the term has had a connotational pejorative bias, so that somehow Smollett appears to be aesthetically inferior to Henry Fielding or Laurence Sterne. If past criticism has not developed an adequate working definition of the grotesque as a useful tool for the analysis of eighteenth-century fiction, the main reason for this failure stems in large part from a mistaken belief that the grotesque is alien to the true comic. One critic finds, for example, that the effect of the grotesque "in which the gruesome and ghastly are offered as purportedly 'funny,' appears increasingly in modern presentations." "But," continues this critic, "when satire loses its lightness and comic effect it ceases to be satire and becomes mere reprimand or criticism" (Marie Collins Swabey, *Comic Laughter: A Philosophical Essay*). The underlying assumption here, that the grotesque is not risible, is linked with another fallacious assumption that satire in order to be risible must not lose its "lightness." When critical theories of the comic dismiss grotesque so that comic satire is emasculated and many of the most powerful examples of grotesque satire, from Swift to Heller, no longer fit into the comic mode, then it is surely time that the theories themselves be modified. The richly rewarding studies of the refinement of irony in Swift, Pope, and Fielding

From *Huntington Library Quarterly* 32, no. 2 (February 1969). © 1969 by *Huntington Library Quarterly*.

need now to be supplemented by studies of the equally effective use of farce and the grotesque in eighteenth-century satire and comic fiction.

The real hindrance to a right understanding of grotesque stems from a critical frame of reference derived from the dramatic modes of tragedy and comedy. Implicit in this frame of reference is a hierarchy of values which sees tragedy as the highest form of art, comedy as somewhat lower, and farce as the lowest dramatic form. In neoclassical criticism grotesque was primarily confined to the plastic arts but was felt to be synonymous with farce as a dramatic form. This connection was drawn by John Dryden:

> There is yet a lower sort of poetry and painting, which is out of nature; for a farce is that in poetry, which *grotesque* is in a picture. The persons and action of a farce are all unnatural, and the manners false, that is, inconsisting with the characters of mankind. Grotesque painting is the just resemblance of this; and Horace begins his *Art of Poetry* by describing such a figure, with a man's head, a horse's neck, the wings of a bird, and a fish's tail; parts of different species jumbled together, according to the mad imagination of the dauber; and the end of all this, as he tells you afterward, to cause laughter: a very monster in a Bartholomew Fair, for the mob to gape at for their two-pence. Laughter is indeed the propriety of a man, but just enough to distinguish him from his elder brother with four legs.
>
>   ("A Parallel of Poetry and Painting Prefixed to the
>   Version of Du Fresnoy, *De Arte Graphica*")

Dryden's objection to farce and the grotesque is that they function on a low or crudely comic level merely to elicit laughter. By implication high comedy functions both to elicit laughter and to stimulate thought. In his preface to *An Evening Love* Dryden praises a high form of comedy for consisting of "natural actions and characters," whereas farce consists of "forced humours, and unnatural events" and "entertains" with "what is monstrous and chimerical." The inadequacy of Dryden's pejorative treatment of farce and its lingering influence in eighteenth-century dramatic theory has been shown by Professor Leo Hughes. Dryden's comparison between farce and grotesque, used later as a defining quotation for *grotesque* in Johnson's *Dictionary,* must have also had a negative influence on eighteenth-century attitudes toward the grotesque. Both farce and grotesque were felt to be inferior forms, and yet these are precisely the forms most characteristic of Smollett's fiction.

Even fairly recent aesthetic criticism has sometimes taken a negative attitude toward the farcical and the grotesque. Martin Foss describes the philosophy of farce as a belief that "chance rules over our life, that nothing really is necessary, that we are faced every moment with a surprising adventure which turns meaning into nonsense." Foss condemns this philosophy as "a distortion of life" and the satisfaction which this distortion gives as "only a pseudo-satisfaction," defining the grotesque as a "more serious variation of farce" in which "discontinuity, chance, surprise" are not "symptoms of a funny world" but of "a sinister world of chaos which the suffering individual is eager to shake off."

> In times of chaos men return to a magic form of art, using the demoniac aspects of life for their stories and plays: sickness, insanity, death; but they turn them into grotesque means for laughter in order to regain their inner balance. . . . The grotesque will always appear and take hold of those ages which are under the strain of disaster, feeling the sinister and chaotic aspects of life, but advanced enough to appease the mind by laughter.
>
> *(Symbol and Metaphor in Human Experience)*

Just when it would seem that Foss is preparing a strong case in favor of the grotesque, he returns to his thesis that "great art, just as great religion, expresses confidence and raises from death and destruction"; and he condemns "the funny and the grotesque" as "both inefficient and futile means to cover up, rather than to heal, the diseases and deficiencies of our existence." Here we are faced with a theory of farce and grotesque that shows a pejorative bias. Foss's assertion that "great art" should heal would hardly seem to fit the best of eighteenth-century English comic, grotesque satire. By Foss's standards, corrosive satire would not be great art, since it could hardly be said to heal. Surely it is enough, however, that satire merely criticizes negatively what is.

II

A positive approach to a working hypothesis of the grotesque in the analysis of literature was provided by Thomas Mann in an essay on Joseph Conrad. The "striking feature of modern art" for Mann is "that it has ceased to recognise the categories of tragic and comic, or the dramatic classifications, tragedy and comedy." Modern art "sees life as tragicomedy," Mann goes on to write, "with the result that the grotesque is its most genuine style—to the extent indeed, that today that is the only guise in which the sublime may appear." "The grotesque is the genuine anti-bourgeois style," Mann asserts, and he believes that "the comic-grotesque" has al-

ways been Anglo-Saxondom's "strong point." Since Mann's seminal essay
was written early in this century, the grotesque has indeed become a vital
mode both in contemporary fiction and theater of the absurd. Recent aesthetic theory has tried to show why the grotesque has become so essential
an element of contemporary art. After observing that tragedy is "the strict-
est genre in art," presupposing "a formed world," whereas comedy "sup-
poses an unformed world," Friedrich Duerrenmatt asserts that "comedy
alone is suitable for us": "Our world has led to the grotesque as well as
to the atom bomb. . . . But the grotesque is only a way of expressing in a
tangible manner, of making us perceive physically the paradoxical, the
form of the unformed, the face of a world without face; and just as in our
thinking today we seem to be unable to do without the concept of the paradox, so also in art, and in our world which at times seems still to exist
only because the atom bomb exists: out of fear of the bomb." This statement by Duerrenmatt is quoted by Albert Hofstadter in his brilliant essay
on the tragicomic. The tragicomic for Hofstadter consists of "the effective
copresence of opposites," the "pathos" and the "comicality," *not* in harmony or resolution, but in an equilibrium of "tension that points to no
possible resolution." Hofstadter sees the tragicomic response as a means
by which "man tries to make possible a living stance toward a grotesque
reality" and he suggests that the "closest we come to the tragic" in contemporary experience "is by the way of the grotesque, that strange borderland
phenomenon." Both Duerrenmatt and Hofstadter seem to suggest that the
real world as we know it is grotesque, so that aesthetic representation of
this real world will itself rely on a mode of the grotesque. Hofstadter distinguishes from the grotesque or tragicomic those "aesthetic types expressive of nihilism" in contemporary art, such as "the purely ugly-disgusting
and the purely farcical nonsensical." Today, then, the grotesque mode is
considered highly functional, highly effective, and highly respectable. Pejorative bias still persists toward the grotesque and the farcical even by objective aestheticians, however, when the grotesque is felt to express nihilis-
tic attitudes.

All of this is pertinent to an understanding of the grotesque in *Humphry Clinker*. A truly great work of literature is always a contemporary
work of literature. We cannot praise the grotesque and the farcical in contemporary literature as meaningful aesthetic modes and then find Smollett
interesting but somewhat inferior to his contemporaries because of his use
of the grotesque and the farcical. A working definition of the grotesque as
well as a useful summary of critical theories on the subject is to be found
in the first chapter of Lee Byron Jennings's *The Ludicrous Demon: Aspects*

of the Grotesque in German Post-Romantic Prose. Jennings rejects the traditional belief that the grotesque is "merely a species of low comedy or some type of extravagant exaggeration or aimless combination of opposites." He finds the psychological locus of grotesque to reside in "the distorting activity of the human imagination" in which "the deepest foundations of our being are interfered with: the stability and constancy of the human form." This "distortion" proceeds "toward chaos or formlessness," in "the borderland" of the imagination "between recognizable and unrecognizable form":

> The grotesque displays something more than the superficial distortion of most caricature, which alters the outlines of a given original and gains its effect by exaggerating a part with respect to the whole; it is rather a distortion that penetrates to the bases of our perception of reality. It is significant that the grotesque figure commonly displays a union of disparate parts from the animal, vegetable, and mineral kingdoms or from the worlds of man and beast. The "original" (the human form in general) is not so much distorted in the strict sense as it is destroyed and rebuilt along new lines. There is a recombining of the elements of experienced reality to form something alien to it; the norms of common life are replaced by an "anti-norm."

Jennings believes that "the grotesque object always displays a *combination of fearsome and ludicrous qualities*" in that "it simultaneously arouses reactions of fear and amusement in the observer." The basic attitude of the observer toward the grotesque object Jennings finds to be "a detached contemplation, characterized by amusement, contempt, and astonishment." For Jennings, the grotesque "represents one of the ways in which humor conquers anxiety and fear" and he defines the grotesque as *"the demonic made trivial"* in which there is "the preservation of the balance between fearsome and ludicrous aspects."

"A grotesque situation" Jennings sees as displaying "a deep-seated distortion with aspects of the fearsome and ludicrous, where absurdity runs rampant," a distortion not comprising "a departure from the human form, but rather a violation of the basic norms of experience pertaining in our daily life":

> Again, the distortion must not proceed to the point of pure senselessness, but must result in the creation of an entirely new ordering principle, an "anti-norm." The customary order of

things must seem to give way to a kind of deranged intent on
the part of nature itself. The current of demonic fear expresses
itself in this case not as the menace of a bogey, but as the collapse of a world. The familiar structure of existence is under-
mined and chaos seems imminent. This aspect is intensified
when concrete manifestations of decay appear and a feeling of
hopelessness and corruption is developed. The ludicrous aspect,
in turn, arises from the farcical quality inherent in such scenes
of absurdity and approaching chaos.

As Jennings remarks much later in his study, the grotesque "represents the
means of coping with the anxieties of an epoch" and "each age has its
demons."

In analyzing the grotesque in *Humphry Clinker,* I should like to use
Jennings's approach as a working critical frame of reference—with one
qualification. Because he defines grotesque in preparation for a study of its
usage by nineteenth-century German writers, Jennings tends to place the
grotesque in a tragicomic borderland and to stress an almost tragic grotesque. I would like to emphasize more what Mann calls the "comic grotesque." I should also like to remove all dramatic antecedents from my
critical frame of reference by placing Smollett's grotesque in the broad,
nondramatic context of *humor.* It is humor that subsumes satire, irony, in-
vective, farce, comedy, and the grotesque, without making implicit value
judgments about the superiority of one device to another. And if by humor
I mean that literary mode which elicits laughter, I do not mean thereby to
sentimentalize humor by separating it from satire. Such a concept of humor as nonsatirical lacks historical justification and is wholly arbitrary.

In *The Intelligencer,* no. 3 (1728), Jonathan Swift anonymously de-
fended John Gay's *Beggar's Opera* against the charge that it was farce or
low comedy by first making a case for humor as a vital comic mode and
then by saying that the play excelled in its humor. In the process of appealing to another mode to defend the play against a classical criterion that
relegated farce or low comedy to an inferior status, Swift asserts that humor "is certainly the best Ingredient towards that Kind of Satyr, which is
most useful, and gives the least Offence; which, instead of lashing, laughs
Men out of their Follies, and Vices; and is the Character that gives *Horace*
the Preference to *Juvenal.*" If not the most vitriolic mode, humor for Swift
can nonetheless be satiric.

Another reason for seeing Smollett's use of the grotesque within the
context of humor is that Smollett was working in a Scottish tradition of

humor, the components of which have been described by Wallace Notestein as "the fantastic or grotesque," satire, and "rollicking high spirits." In his discussion of Robert Henryson, Kurt Wittig refers to "grotesque exaggeration" and to "the juxtaposition of understatement and overstatement" as characteristic of Scottish literature. Ernest Baker also observes that Smollett has "that particular touch of acrid Scottish humour to be recognized in his compatriots Hawes and Dunbar, in the past, and in Charles Johnstone, Burns, and Byron a little later." Smollett himself provides a clue in *Humphry Clinker* to the Scottish source of his humor. Jery Melford describes his repartee with Lieutenant Lismahago after he has suggested that the Scots are "generally supposed little subject to the impressions of humour." Lismahago retorts that the English could not judge this as they did not understand Scottish dialect "in common discourse, as well as in their works of humour." When Melford asks what these works of humor are, Lismahago refers him to *The Ever-green* and to the works of Allan Ramsay and complains that the North-Briton is seen to a disadvantage in an English company because his dialect and vocabulary are not understood: the North-Briton "therefore finds himself *under a restraint, which is a great enemy to wit and humour* [italics mine]." Although these words are spoken in a comic context in which Lismahago is partly an object of ridicule, still Smollett has provided an interior norm for understanding his own brand of humor and grotesque which *is* most effective when least restrained.

Etymologically, there is also strong justification for relating the grotesque in *Humphry Clinker* to the spectrum of humor. In Samuel Johnson's *Dictionary* (1773) "humorous" in its first sense is defined as "Full of grotesque or odd images," and in its third sense as "Pleasant; jocular." Both senses are fused in Johnson's fifth definition of "humour" as "Grotesque imagery; jocularity; merriment." Johnson's definition could not contain, however, the newer meanings of the comic grotesque just in the process of being discovered and discussed by Continental critics. In his *Discours sur la poésie dramatique* included in the first printed edition of *Le Père de famille* (Amsterdam, 1758), Diderot mentions the relationship between *commedia dell'arte*, with its caricatures, and the grotesque engravings of Jacques Callot. Diderot thereby yokes the grotesque to what he calls "farce excellente." In 1761 Justus Möser published a pamphlet defending the grotesque as a legitimate aesthetic mode. Like Diderot, Möser turned to the world of the *commedia dell'arte* to support his defense. In 1766, at just about the time Smollett may have begun *Humphry Clinker,* Möser's pamphlet was translated into English and published in London as

Harlequin: or, a Defence of Grotesque Comic Performances. Not only Smollett, then, but his readers as well had had some opportunity to become familiar with the Continental discussion of comic grotesque. If Smollett started out to experiment with a somewhat shallower form of comic grotesque as contrasted with its more profound treatment in later European writers such as Jean Paul, *Humphry Clinker* in its final form presents a strikingly modern, complex grotesque, the texture and significance of which will be examined in the rest of this paper.

III

Jennings (with the support of Thomas Mann and other students of the grotesque) insists that the results of the grotesque "are entirely concrete" and that the term can only be meaningfully applied in aesthetic analysis to "particular objects or figures." *Humphry Clinker* is perhaps the most grotesque work in all of eighteenth-century English literature, and Jennings's definitions will enable us to see how grotesque objects and situations in the novel function specifically and concretely and how they relate to its total meaning.

If, as Jennings writes, the grotesque "represents the means of coping with the anxieties of an epoch" and each epoch "has its demons," the demon imagery in *Humphry Clinker* can be shown to be an integral part of the novel's grotesque. Certain of the characters' anxieties are embodied in their demonic projections. Matthew Bramble is early established as both a *vir bonum* and as a profoundly disturbed man. He is "equally distressed in mind and body" and suffers from a morbid imagination. Hence his comic-grotesque vision may be explained away as being merely pathological. But if, as Jung says, "not only does the psyche exist, it is existence itself," then the reality of Matthew's grotesque vision is a fact of the fictional context and as disturbing to the reader as if the real world itself were indeed grotesque. From the very beginning Matthew complains about his demons: "the dæmon of vapours" descending "in a perpetual drizzle on Clifton-Downs" and Tabitha Bramble as "the *devil incarnate* come to torment" him "for his sins" [italics mine]. The new buildings of Bath look to Matthew as if "*some Gothic devil* [italics mine] had stuffed them altogether in a bag, and left them to stand higgledy piggledy, just as chance directed." He condemns ale, gin, and the "trashy family of made wines" as "*infernal compositions* [italics mine], contrived for the destruction of the human species." Later after reducing a "polite" assembly of Bath to "*a compound of villainous smells*" arising from "putrid gums, inposthumated lungs, sour

flutulencies, rank arm-pits, sweating feet, running sores and issues, plas-
ters, ointments, and embrocations, hungary-water, spirit of lavendar," etc.,
Matthew bewails his ever having left Wales for Bath—"I wonder what the
devil [italics mine] possessed me." The breakdown of social degree and
subordination in London, Matthew attributes to "the demons of profligacy
and licentiousness." In a satanic world, Matthew believes that the king of
England is "too good for the times" and that a "king of England should
have a spice of the devil in his constitution." Finally, Matthew complains
that even literature and taste are dominated by "virulent factions," that
"every department of life" has been unsurped by "the dæmon of party."

Winifred Jenkins has her demons. For her, the area of anxiety revolves
around sex. That the carnival or circus "often serves as the background
for a grotesque situation" Jennings believes is "partly because of its affinity
for freaks and monstrous masked figures and partly because of its radical
departure from the conventions of everyday life, its creations of a fantastic
world in which standards of identity and seriousness no longer apply." A
grotesque situation involving Winifred occurs when she visits the Tower to
see the wild beasts. She is jokingly warned not to go near the cage of a
"monstracious lion, with teeth half a quarter long" because he would roar
if she was not a virgin. (He roars.) Afterwards, Winifred goes to a "party
at Sadler's-wells," where she "saw such tumbling and dancing upon ropes
and wires" that she "was frightened, and ready to go into a fit," thought
"it was all inchantment," and thinking herself "bewitched, began for to
cry." Comparing the acrobats to "witches in Wales" flying upon broom-
sticks, Winifred is certain "they must deal with the devil": "A fine gentleman, with a pig's-tail, and a golden sord by his side, came to comfit me,
and offered for to treat me with a pint of wind; but I would not stay; and
so, in *going through the dark passage, he began to shew his cloven futt*
[italics mine], and went for to be rude. . . ." The gentleman is converted
by Winifred's imagination into a demon, while her unconscious sexual de-
sires are projected as phallic symbols. Smollett's consistency and his conscious use of the grotesque is shown when much later in the narrative Winifred writes to Mrs. Mary Jones that she has "been a vixen and a *griffin*
[italics mine] these many days" and that "Sattin has had power to tempt"
her in "the shape of van Ditton, the young 'squire's wally de shamble; but
by God's grease he did not purvail."

Even Humphry projects this demon out of his religious enthusiasm.
Lydia, unhappy in love, goes to the Tabernacle, hears a discourse, prays
"fervently to be enlightened," and then begins to be "in terrible apprehen-
sions about the state" of her "poor soul" because she is not yet sensible of

"inward motions, those operations of grace, which are the signs of a regen-erated spirit." It is at this Tabernacle that Humphry has been preaching. Finally, Matthew Bramble confronts Humphry, who admits he has had an inward admonition of the spirit. "An admonition of the devil," the squire retorts, and then warns Humphry about the dangers of being a "wrong-headed enthusiast":

> "if you are really seduced by the reveries of a disturbed imagi-nation, the sooner you lose your senses entirely, the better for yourself and the community. In that case, some charitable per-son might provide you with a dark room and clean straw in Bedlam, where it would not be in your power to infect others with your fanaticism; whereas, if you have just reflection enough left to maintain the character of a chosen vessel in the meetings of the godly, you and your hearers will be misled by a Will-i'-the wisp, from one error into another, till you are plunged into religious frenzy; and then, perhaps, you will hang yourself in despair."

Behind this passage lie the sad cases of Smart and Collins; and, contempo-raneous to it, the religious despair of William Cowper. The "affrighted Clinker" admits that he "may be under the temptation of the devil," who wants to "wreck" him "on the rocks of spiritual pride." Later, after Hum-phry has been placed in jail and the turnkey complains that Humphry "deals with the devil," Jery Melford enters the prison and sees a "strongly picturesque" scene of Humphry preaching to a group of chained felons, the faces exhibiting a "variety of attention" that would "not have dis-graced the pencil of a Raphael."

Jennings's observation that the grotesque figure frequently "displays a union of disparate parts from the animal, vegetable, and mineral kingdoms or from the worlds of man and beast" is demonstrated by a number of grotesque figures in *Humphry Clinker*. Jery Melford's letter contains the anecdote about Tim Cropdale, who, seeing a creditor approaching with a raised cane, metamorphoses himself "into a miserable blind wretch, feeling his way with a long stick from post to post, and rolling about two bald unlighted orbs instead of eyes." This metamorphosis satirizes the obsession of the later eighteenth century with universal benevolence (Cropdale is a hack writer who has written a "virgin tragedy"). Cropdale becomes sym-bolically analogous to the grotesque trickster or the ludicrous demon. This interpretation is confirmed when in the next paragraph he is described as taking his repose "during the heats of summer" upon "a bulk" or indulging "himself, in fresco, with one of the kennel-nymphs, under the portico of St. Martin's church." The bookseller cries out that if Cropdale had stolen his whip and spurs he would have probably stolen another horse and "then he would have *rid to the devil of course*" [italics mine]. Smollett's comparing Cropdale's antics to the frescoes of ludicrous demons performing obscene antics, coupled with the allusion to the Gothic devil quoted earlier, is unmistakable evidence that Smollett was consciously working with the grotesque mode.

The grotesque situation is an extreme situation. Matthew's morbid imagination and anxiety marks his confrontation with approaching death; it is his fear and trembling converted into a sardonic humorous vision that is at the heart of his "sportive grotesque." His description of some old friends in a Bath coffeehouse converts potential anxiety over death into grotesque figures:

> We consisted of thirteen individuals; seven lamed by the gout, rheumatism, or palsy; three maimed by accident; and the rest either deaf or blind. One hobbled, another hopped, a third dragged his legs after him like a wounded snake, a fourth straddled betwixt a pair of long crutches, like the mummy of a felon hanging in chains; a fifth was bent into a horizontal position, like a mounted telescope, shoved in by a couple of chairmen; and a sixth was the bust of a man, set upright in a wheel machine, which the waiter moved from place to place.

This grotesque distortion is reinforced by mechanical objectifications of the human form, by a kind of synecdoche bordering on metonymy: "The *bust* was what remained of colonel Cockril, who had lost the use of his limbs in making an American campaign; and the *telescope* proved to be my college chum, sir Reginald Bentley [italics mine]." These grotesque death-in-life figures render death trivial, and Matthew suggests that his "enjoyment was not the less pleasing for being mixed with a strain of melancholy, produced by the remembrance of past scenes, that conjured up the ideas of some endearing connexions, which the hand of Death has actually dissolved." Dehumanized by war, Colonel Cockril foreshadows the most grotesque figure in *Humphry Clinker*—Lieutenant Lismahago. Here, one must recognize that the atrocities of Indian frontier warfare reported in eighteenth-century British periodicals would have had much the same grim effect on readers as recent atrocities reported in the Congo would have on readers today. Lismahago's Thurberlike mythic reduction of Indian captivity converts English anxieties about Indian massacres to a ludicrous, demonic myth. By all rights Lismahago should be dead, having been "rifled," "scalped," and left for dead with a broken skull by the Indians. His skull "left naked in several places" and covered "with patches" makes him reminiscent of the skeleton in the dance of death. The skeleton's dance of death Jennings finds a "prime example of the grotesque situation" in which "the menace of decay and the collapse of our existence" is ameliorated by "the farcical element" of the "ludicrous figure" of the human skeleton. Indeed, Jery Melford describes Lismahago and his horse as "a resurrection of dry bones," and he learns that the lieutenant "had been wounded, maimed, mutilated, taken, and enslaved." At the conclusion of *Humphry Clinker* a farce is got up in which Jack Wilson plays Harlequin Skeleton and Lismahago, Pierrot. Lismahago is "peculiarly adapted to his part" so that "when the skeleton held him in chase, his horror became most divertingly picturesque." Jery reports that it was such "a lively representation of Death in pursuit of Consumption," some of the spectators "shrieked aloud, and others ran out of the hall in the utmost consternation." This is followed in the next paragraph by Jery's description of the arrival of Lismahago's "long dealbox" from London, *"not unlike a coffin"* [italics mine]. Finally, as Lismahago marches to the altar at his wedding, there is "a languishing leer upon his countenance, in which there seemed to be something arch and ironical." Jennings has observed that in Dürer's representation of the Devil or in the gargoyles of Gothic cathedrals there is a "characteristic bestial leer of the face" that "expresses idiotic clownishness as well as demonic malevolence." If Matthew's vision is grotesque, then Lismahago by Jery Melford's account is the grotesque figure in real life. It has not been sufficiently recognized how Lismahago's tirades on commerce's corruption of society and its "universal anarchy" parody Matthew's own tirades on the social anarchy of Bath and London. Lismahago as a therapeutic foil helps to ameliorate Matthew's mobid imagination in that as the living grotesque object, Lismahago serves as a catharsis for Matthew's grotesque views in the literal modern psychiatric sense of alleviating the squire's fears and anxieties by bringing them to consciousness and giving them objectivity.

IV

It is all too easy to rationalize away the corrosiveness of Matthew's satire, and by doing so, force it into the "dialect of compromise." [The phrase is Ronald Paulson's.] Obviously, other points of view qualify Matthew's vision, and certainly its grim grotesquerie diminishes as his psychosomatic condition improves. But neither does Bramble return to Bath and London. In spite of the contextual qualification, Matthew's early grotesque vision, like Gulliver's, remains disturbingly convincing. For me, at any rate, after *Humphry Clinker* is read the grotesque passages linger—profound, corrosive, and enduring. Horace Walpole apparently felt so when he contemptuously dismissed *Humphry Clinker* as "a party novel, written by the profligate hireling Smollett, to vindicate the Scots." If Walpole's criticism is a gross oversimplification (a refusal to see Scotland as an agrarian, pastoral symbol satirizing urban, mechanistic, pathological London and Bath society), there is a great deal of truth in his recognizing the political ethos of the work. Smollett's social satire expressed through Matthew relies in part on a submerged metaphor of urban society as a diseased organism. It is a metaphor stemming from Plato's *Republic:* "Justice is produced in the soul, like health in the body, by establishing the elements concerned in their natural relations of control and subordination, wheareas injustice is like disease and means that this natural order is inverted." Merely because Matthew is pathologically disturbed does not exclude the possibility that English society is itself pathological. The grotesque "current of demonic fear," according to Jennings, may express itself "as the collapse of a world," and "the farcical quality" grows out of "scenes of absurdity" inherent in "approaching chaos." The world that has collapsed for Matthew Bramble is the English Augustan world. His satire on London and Bath echoes Jonathan Swift: he refers to an "open bason in the Circus, liable to be defiled with dead dogs, cats, rats, and every species of nastiness, which the rascally populace may throw into it, from mere wantonness and brutality." And there is an obviously Swiftian tone to Matthew's vision, to his seeing Bath as a "national hospital" for "lunatics," and to his condemnation of chaotic society as a monstrous mob.

Matthew's grotesque vision is shockingly concrete and detailed. It jolts the senses. Jery describes Matthew as possessing "delicacy of feeling," as "extravagantly delicate in all his sensations, both of soul and body." Tim Cropdale, a kind of literary con man, is described as having once lived by writing novels until "that branch of business" was "engrossed by female authors" who published "merely for the propagation of virtue, with so much ease and spirit, *and delicacy,* and knowledge of the human heart, and all in the *severe tranquillity of high life,* that the reader is not only *enchanted* [italics mine] by their genius, but reformed by their morality." Delicacy as "exquisite fineness of feeling" and a "refined sense of what is becoming, modest or proper" (*OED*) had become the primary motivating norm for later eighteenth-century fiction, so that the emphasis on sensibility had turned into a cult of hedonistic feeling. In his *Philosophical Enquiry into the Origin of Our Ideas of the Sublime and Beautiful,* Edmund Burke had distinguished between the sublime and the beautiful so that, in J. T. Boulton's words, beauty was left "a weak and sentimentalized conception," a "mere prettiness"; and section 16 of Burke's *Enquiry* was devoted to "Delicacy" as a quality of the beautiful. Matthew's *disenchanting* comic grotesque functions in part as anti-delicate; and in that Burke insisted on terror and deliberate obscurity as contributing to the sublime, the clarity and concreteness of the grotesque in *Humphry Clinker* operates as anti-sublime. If, as Boulton observes, Burke's marked emphasis was on defining beauty in terms of an "uncompromising sensationism," Smollett's use of the grotesque makes such *delicate* sensationism untenable.

Humphry Clinker represents Smollett's last great defense of the empirical comic view of life with all its concomitant aesthetic values. It should be compared with William Hogarth's last print, "Tailpiece, or the Bathos" (April 1764), which has been called "the epilogue to the Augustan age." The caption of Hogarth's print, "THE BATHOS, *or Manner of Sinking, in Sublime Paintings, Inscribed to the Dealers in Dark Pictures,*" is qualified by a footnote which reads: *"See the manner of disgracing ye most Serious Subjects, in many celebrated Old Pictures; by introducing Low, absurd, obscene & often prophane Circumstances into them."* The footnote clearly refers to the grotesque in baroque paintings. Father Time as he expires leaves a will in which atoms are consigned to *"Chaos whom I appoint my sole Executor."* Professor Ronald Paulson interprets the print as "the culmination of such pessimistic images as the overturning of Britannia's coach, and the changes made in earlier prints—the seal of England added to the wall of Bedlam, the British lion's teeth removed, and Comedy turned into Tragedy." Paulson perceptively observes that Hogarth was parodying aesthetic values in painting and theory systematized by Burke and that Hogarth used "the very images" he attacks *"as* images to express his pessimistic statement about the condition of England and the world governed by such values." Extreme pessimism framed in a comic setting so that the pessimism is qualified, yet not one iota diminished, is the ultimate function of the grotesque in *Humphry Clinker.*

There is no real resolution in *Humphry Clinker.* The happy ending is a surface one, ironically and deliberately so. Unless we read *Humphry Clinker* with the very sentimental delicacy Smollett was satirizing, the plot resolution has all the sardonic superficiality of the conclusions to Hemingway's *The Sun Also Rises,* when in answer to Lady Brett's "Oh, Jake, we could have had such a damned good time together," Jake replies: "Yes, isn't it *pretty* [italics mine] to think so?" What dominates *Humphry Clinker* is Matthew's early grotesque vision, even as *Travels into Several Remote Nations of the World* is dominated by Gulliver's corrosive, Yahoo vision of mankind. Yet just as Gulliver's vexing vision exists among a complexity of multiple points of view in a fictional context so that Gulliver is both satirizer and satirized, Matthew Bramble's vision operates in the same way in *Humphry Clinker*. Both Swift and Smollett recognized the value of self-parody, of self-awareness, of qualifying one's satire by recognizing its limitation in the perspective of time. Wolfgang Kayser distinguishes between caricature and the true grotesque by seeing caricature as primarily satirical and didactic, whereas the grotesque represents an underlying sense of cultural and cosmic disintegration and chaos. Kayser's example of this distinction is Hogarth's *Gin Lane* where most of the details are polemical (to show the danger of gin) except for the collapsing houses, which Kayser sees as providing the grotesque perspective of a world going to pieces. There are, no doubt, scenes and descriptions in *Humphry Clinker* that represent caricature rather than the grotesque. But I would conclude that because Smollett's use of the grotesque is more integrated, functional, and profound in *Humphry Clinker* than in any of his previous works, it is Smollett's most successful novel.

T. O. TREADWELL

The Two Worlds
of Ferdinand Count Fathom

Two conflicting views of the function of the heroes of novels may be seen to have been held by English writers and critics throughout the 1750s. The principle that the purpose of fiction, whether in prose or verse, is to imitate human nature, was unquestioned, but as to the fidelity of imitation proper in the novel a dispute arose. It was argued on the one hand that the novelist ought to represent human nature as it is commonly observed in the world. This may involve the depiction of "low" characters and actions, but it will provide an accurate guide to the temptations and dangers likely to be encountered in the journey through life. William Park has pointed to John Cleland's 1751 review of *Peregrine Pickle,* which provides an excellent summary of this position:

> If we consider then in general, before we come to particular application, the true use of these writings [comic romances], it is more to be lamented that we have so few of them, than that there are too many. For as the matter of them is chiefly taken from nature, from adventures, real or imaginary, but familiar, practical, and probable to be met with in the course of common life, they may serve as pilot's charts, or maps of those parts of the world, which every one may chance to travel through; and in this light they are public benefits. Whereas romances and novels which turn upon characters out of nature, monsters of perfection, feats of chivalry, fairy-enchantments, and the whole

From *Tobias Smollett: Bicentennial Essays Presented to Lewis M. Knapp,* edited by G. S. Rousseau and P.-G. Boucé. © 1971 by Oxford University Press.

train of the marvellous-absurd, transport the reader unprofit-
ably into the clouds, where he is sure to find no common footing, or into those wilds of fancy, which go for ever out of the
way of all human paths.

For those who share this view, the effectiveness of the novel as a "pilot's
chart" allowed any sort of material, however "low," to be brought within
its scope. Thus Ralph Griffiths can praise Cleland's own *Memoirs of Fanny
Hill* as a morally improving work because it shows in their true light the
pitfalls that await the unwary:

> The author of *Fanny Hill* does not seem to have expressed any
> thing with a view to countenance the practice of any immorali-
> ties, but meerly to exhibit truth and nature to the world, and
> to lay open those mysteries of iniquity that, in our opinion,
> need only to be exposed to view, in order to their being ab-
> horred and shunned by those who might otherwise unwarily
> fall into them. . . . Vice has indeed fair quarter allowed it; and
> after painting whatever charms it may pretend to boast, with
> the fairest impartiality, the supposed female author concludes
> with a lively declaration in favour of sobriety, temperance, and
> virtue.

Cleland and Griffiths emphasize the didactic effectiveness of plot—the ability of the novelist to expose his characters to the snares set for virtue in
the world, and by this means to warn his readers against them. Another
group of novelists and critics were concerned with the potency of fictional
characters—the creation by the novelist of models to be imitated. The
clearest expression of this view is probably to be found in Samuel Johnson's fourth *Rambler* (1750):

> Many writers, for the sake of following nature, so mingle good
> and bad qualities in their principal personages, that they are
> both equally conspicuous; and as we accompany them through
> their adventures with delight, and are led by degrees to interest
> ourselves in their favour, we lose the abhorrence of their faults,
> because they do not hinder our pleasure, or, perhaps, regard
> them with some kindness, for being united with so much
> merit. . . . In narratives, where historical veracity has no place,
> I cannot discover why there should not be exhibited the most
> perfect idea of virtue; of virtue not angelical, nor above proba-
> bility, for what we cannot credit, we shall never imitate, but the
> highest and purest that humanity can reach, which, exercised in

such trials as the various revolutions of things shall bring upon it, may, by conquering some calamities, and enduring others, teach us what we may hope, and what we can perform.

Johnson's opinion was probably in Samuel Richardson's mind when, in "A Concluding note by the editor" appended to the last volume of *The History of Sir Charles Grandison* (1753–54), he admitted that, "Human Nature as it *is*," is indeed sometimes corrupt, but asked, "need pictures of this be held out in books?"

The adoption of one or the other of these theories about the didactic aim of the novel has an obvious reflection in the final form of the work. If the novel is conceived as a chart for guiding the reader safely through the shoals and rapids of villainy, then it must clearly expose its heroes and heroines to as many of the assaults and temptations of the villainous as is consistent with probability. It will thus be episodic and geographically discursive, following its characters up and down the social scale as they are punished or rewarded for their conduct in the adventures through which they pass. If the novel sets out to exhibit a virtuous man or woman for the edification and imitation of its readers, its range will be deeper and less broad. Its ambience will be rather domestic than peripatetic, and it will develop through the interaction of a relatively small number of characters with one another, rather than through their reactions to the environments in which they find themselves. It is to these formal aspects of the two theories of the role of the novel that Johnson referred when, speaking of Fielding and Richardson, he distinguished between "characters of manners" and "characters of nature." "Characters of manners are very entertaining; but they are to be understood, by a more superficial observer, than characters of nature, where a man must dive into the recesses of the human heart."

These differing views on the proper portrayal of human nature in the novel underlie the quarrel between the partisans of Richardson and Fielding which occupied the English novel-reading public throughout the middle years of the eighteenth century, and there can be little doubt that the publication of *Roderick Random* in 1748 placed Smollett squarely among the novelists who were seen to paint "Human Nature as it *is*." Martin Battestin has drawn attention to a pamphlet published in 1748 which, while highly praising *Joseph Andrews*, find that *Random* too faithfully pictures the grosser aspects of human nature. "There are many free Strokes that please, because they are true and agreeable to Nature; but some Truths are not to be told, and the most skilful Painters represent Nature with a Veil." Catherine Talbot, in a letter to Elizabeth Carter dated February 15, 1748, speaks of "that strange book *Roderick Random*! It is a very strange and a very low one, though not without some characters in it, and I believe some very just, though very wretched descriptions." Smollett had anticipated this sort of reaction from some of his readers, and he included in the preface to *Random* a justification for the "mean scenes" in which his hero is engaged on the grounds that the "humours and passions" can be observed more clearly when they are "undisguised by affectation, ceremony, or education." Roderick himself, although labeled by his creator an embodiment of "modest merit," clearly does not represent the highest and purest form of virtue that humanity can reach. Still less so does the hero of *Peregrine Pickle* (1751), or the unfortunate Lady Vane, whose interpolated "Memoirs," as Howard S. Buck has shown, attracted most of the attention which Smollett's second novel received. Summarizing the contemporary reaction to the first two novels, a student of the history of Smollett's reputation writes, "Thus at the very beginning we find two notes struck—Smollett's fidelity to life and his lowness—whose variations seem to have been inexhaustible." That *Random* and *Pickle,* especially the former, were hugely popular is undeniable, but it is equally clear that they were seen to fall into that class of novels which dealt with human nature as it is rather than as it ought to be, and that they were condemned accordingly by those who took the other view of the responsibility of the novelist.

Modern critics have tended to emphasize the essential similarity between the novels of Richardson and Fielding, and have pointed out that most ordinary readers throughout the latter half of the eighteenth century enjoyed reading the novels of both schools. Nevertheless, it seems clear that, while *Tom Jones* and *Roderick Random* were very widely read, the weight of critical opinion inclined toward the Johnsonian, or Richardsonian, view of the novel.

It is in the context of this critical climate that the form and structure of Smollett's third novel, *The Adventures of Ferdinand Count Fathom,* must be approached, for it represents not so much a continuation or a mutation of the techniques established in the first two novels as it does a reaction to the criticism those novels had attracted. As a result, *Fathom* can be read as a unique, if not altogether successful, attempt to combine within one book the didactic techniques of the novel of manners and the novel of nature. That Smollett had been stung by those critics who had dismissed *Random* and *Pickle* as "low" works may be inferred from the long and bitter apostrophe which he inserted into the first chapter of *Fathom:*

And here it will not be amiss to anticipate the remarks of the reader, who, in the chastity and excellency of his conception, may possibly exclaim, "Good Heaven! will these authors never reform their imaginations, and lift their ideas from the obscene objects of low life? Must the publick be again disgusted with the groveling adventures of a waggon? Will no writer of genius draw his pen in the vindication of taste, and entertain us with the agreeable characters, the dignified conversation, the poignant repartee, in short, the genteel comedy of the polite world?"

Have a little patience, gentle, delicate, sublime, critic; you, I doubt not, are one of those consummate connoisseurs, who in their purifications, let humour evaporate, while they endeavour to preserve decorum, and polish wit, until the edge of it is quite wore off; or, perhaps of that class, who, in the sapience of taste, are disgusted with those very flavours, in the productions of their own country, which have yielded infinite delectation to their faculties, when imported from another clime; and damn an author in despite of all precedent and prescription.

Yes, refined reader, we are hastening to that goal of perfection, where satire dares not shew her face; where nature is castigated, almost even to still life; where humour turns changeling, and slavers in an insipid grin; where wit is volatilized into a meer vapour; where decency, divested of all substance, hovers about like a fantastic shadow; where the salt of genius, escaping, leaves nothing but pure and simple phlegm; and the inoffensive pen for ever drops the mild manna of soul-sweetning praise.

These caustic and sarcastic effusions can be said, at least, to show the kind of criticism by which Smollett had been wounded, and the plan of *Fathom,* as outlined in the preface, can be seen to be consciously heroic in response to it. The plan is conceived, to begin with, in dramatic terms. Smollett justifies his use of a villainous protagonist by appealing to the precedents of Shakespeare's Richard III and Congreve's Maskwell, contrasting them with, "Almost all the heroes of this kind, who have hitherto succeeded on the English stage." Evil characters like Fathom, Smollett goes on to say, are didactically effective because the vision of their downfall and punishment arouses in the reader the impulse of fear, "which is the most violent and interesting of all the passions," and which is therefore obviously to be taken seriously (the serious tenor of the passage is reinforced by the echo of Aristotle in the idea). Opposed to the evil protagonist, and counterbalancing the fearful emotions which his fate is designed to provoke, is a hero figure, the embodiment of the virtues, whose function is to "amuse the fancy, engage the affection, and form a striking contrast which might heighten the expression, and give a *Relief* to the moral of the whole." A summary of the didactic motives underlying the novel concludes the preface:

> If I have not succeeded in my endeavours to unfold the myster-
> ies of fraud, to instruct the ignorant, and entertain the vacant;
> if I have failed in my attempts to subject folly to ridicule, and
> vice to indignation; to rouse the spirit of mirth, wake the soul
> of compassion, and touch the secret springs that move the
> heart; I have at least, adorned virtue with honour and applause;
> branded iniquity with reproach and shame, and carefully
> avoided every hint or expression which could give umbrage to
> the most delicate readers.

Both moral techniques receive mention here. The novel fulfills the function of a pilot's chart or map in order to "unfold the mysteries of fraud," but the novelist intends also to "touch the secret springs that move the heart," to produce, that is, a novel of nature in Johnsonian terms. Since Smollett has chosen to make his protagonist a villain, and to balance him schemati- cally with a virtuous deuteragonist, the two techniques which we have called those of manners and of nature will polarize themselves accordingly, the villain assuming by example the didactic function of warning the un- wary against the artifices of his kind and instructing the ignorant in the way of the world, while the hero can be left to assume the role demanded by Johnson and Richardson, exhibiting "the most perfect idea of virtue" for the edification of the judicious. This polarization is, as we should ex- pect, the principle upon which the novel is constructed. *Fathom* encom- passes two fictional worlds, which correspond to the didactic functions which the two chief characters fulfill. At certain points in the story the two worlds touch each other, but the reconciliation of one with the other is morally impossible, given a fictional universe in which good must triumph and evil be punished. These two worlds within the novel are built around the figures of Fathom, the villain, and Renaldo, Count de Melvil, the hero, and they may conveniently be labeled the "world of satire" and the "world of romance."

I have called the fictional milieu in which Fathom's adventures take place "satiric" because the manner in which it fulfills its moral purpose corresponds approximately to the technique of satire, although satire itself is only one of the elements involved in it. This is the world in which Smol- lett endeavors "to unfold the mysteries of fraud, to instruct the ignorant, and entertain the vacant." It encompasses a good part of Europe, ranging up and down the social scale. It has a characteristic diction of its own, the chief element of which is irony. It is a public world, the characters who move within it functioning not as individuals but as members of society.

The world of romance within the novel contains characters who are either heroic and good from the start or who suffer heroically and learn goodness as a result. It is consequently equipped to provide models of good conduct for the reader to emulate. Like the satiric world, it is geographically far-ranging, but its scale is much narrower. It is a private world, and the few characters inhabiting it are drawn from society's upper ranks. The diction in which it is described is hyperbolical and ornate.

Fathom's particular kind of villainy, as M. A. Goldberg has pointed out, owes less to Milton's Satan than to Hobbes and Mandeville; that is to say that his evil deeds are not self-generating and self-sufficient, but rely for their effectiveness on the cupidity and corruption of the society in which he moves. We learn of Fathom that:

> He had formerly imagined, but was now fully persuaded, that the sons of men preyed upon one another, and such was the end and condition of their being. Among the principal figures of life, he observed few or no characters that did not bear a strong analogy to the savage tyrants of the wood. One resembled a tyger in fury and rapaciousness; a second prowled about like a hungry wolf, seeking whom he might devour; a third acted the part of a jackall, in beating the bush for game to his voracious employer; and a fourth imitated the wily fox, in practising a thousand crafty ambuscades for the destruction of the ignorant and and [sic] unwary. The last was the department of life for which he found himself best qualified, by nature and inclination, and he accordingly resolved that his talent should not rust in his possession.

The more corrupt the society in which he finds himself, therefore, and the more ignorant its members, the more scope Fathom will have for the exercise of his capacities, and the society in which he is most successful, and which therefore becomes the hub of the satiric world within the novel, is England.

The idea of foreignism is crucial in *Fathom*, and the mindless contempt with which aliens are treated by Englishmen provokes an undercurrent of bitterness which runs throughout the novel, and which must have its source in Smollett's experience as a Scotsman in London. That he felt himself to be an alien in England, at least during his early years of residence there, can be inferred from *Fathom*, and is stated explicitly in a letter from Smollett to his friend Alexander Carlyle, written in 1753, the year in which *Fathom* was published:

> I do not think I could enjoy life with greater relish in any part of the World than in Scotland among you and your friends . . . I am heartily tired of this land of indifference and phligm where the finer sensations of the soul are not felt, and felicity is held to consist in stupifying Port and overgrown buttocks of Beef— Where Genius is lost, learning undervalued, Taste altogether extinguished, and Ignorance prevail, to such a degree that one of our Chelsea club asked me if the Weather was good when I crossed the sea from Scotland, and another desired to know if there were not more Popes than One, in as much as he had heard people mention the Pope of Rome, an expression which seemed to imply that there was a Pope of some other place.

The first English citizen to appear in *Fathom*, apart from Fathom's mother, a camp-follower who supplements her earnings by killing and robbing the wounded after a battle, is a visitor to Paris, and Smollett begins his description of him by emphasizing that his suspicious xenophobia is not a personal idiosyncrasy, but a national characteristic:

> The baronet's disposition seemed to be cast in the true English mould. He was sour, silent and contemptuous; his very looks indicated a consciousness of superior wealth, and he never opened his mouth, except to make some dry, sarcastic, national reflection: nor was his behaviour free from that air of suspicion which a man puts on, when he believes himself in a croud of pickpockets whom his caution and vigilance set at defiance.

The theme of English xenophobia is reintroduced when Fathom, having at length arrived in the land of his ancestors, boards the London stage-coach at Canterbury. His fellow passengers, "understanding the sixth seat was engaged by a foreigner, determined to profit by his ignorance," and, "with that politeness which is peculiar to this happy island," they make him the victim of a practical joke. The rude insularity of Englishmen is referred to most specifically by Fathom's accomplice, Ratchkali, the Tyrolese gamester. The passage is interesting because it emphasizes the inclusion of the Scots and Irish among those whom the English despise as "foreign." We are surely very close to Smollett's own experience here:

One would imagine, that nature had created the inhabitants, for the support and enjoyment of adventurers like you and me. Not that these islanders open the arms of hospitality to all foreigners without distinction: on the contrary, they inherit from their fathers, an unreasonable prejudice against all nations under the sun; and when an Englishman happens to quarrel with a stranger, the first term of reproach he uses, is the name of his antagonist's country, characterized by some opprobrious epithet; such as a chattering Frenchman, an Italian ape, a German hog, and a beastly Dutchman; nay, their national prepossession is maintained even against those people with whom they are united, under the same laws and government; for, nothing is more common than to hear them exclaim against their fellow-subjects, in the expressions of a beggarly Scot, and an impudent Irish bog-trotter.

Ratchkali goes on to point out how this aspect of the English character can be turned to the confidence-man's advantage, the sense of national superiority thus undermining itself and so containing within itself the seeds of the satirist's revenge. That England is the chief goal and haven of the adventurers of Europe has been stressed throughout. It is, "the land of promise, flowing with milk and honey, and abounding with subjects on which [Fathom] knew his talents would be properly exercised . . . the Canaan of all able adventurers." The biblical parallel is repeated later in the volume when Fathom, from the harbor of Boulogne, "surveyed the neighbouring coast of England, with fond and longing eyes, like another Moses reconnoitring the land of Canaan from the top of mount Pisgah." Like Caesar, however, Fathom has difficulty getting ashore after his voyage. He slips while leaping out of the boat which has carried him ashore, and his hands, appropriately enough, are the first parts of him to touch this promised land. "Upon this occasion, he, in imitation of Scipio's behaviour on the cost [sic] of Afric, hailed the omen, and grasping an handful of the sand, was heard to exclaim in the Italian language, 'Ah ha, old England, I have thee fast.'" Some of the qualities that render the English, as described by Ratchkali, the prime dupes of Europe are laudable ones: honesty makes them credulous, for example, and love of privacy keeps them from prying, but these excellencies of character are not apparent in Fathom's experience as his career develops.

For England turns out to be somewhat different from the paradise of gullibility imagined by Fathom and described by the Tyrolese, and among her citizens are found the crafty and vicious as well as the credulous and simple. The English in *Fathom* are either fools or knaves, and the two qualities are united and summarized in the splendid figure of Sir Stentor Stile, one of the finest of Smollett's grotesques:

> While [Fathom] thus enjoyed his pre-heminence, together with the fruits of success at play, which he managed so discreetly, as never to incur the reputation of an adventurer; he one day, chanced to be at the ordinary, when the company was surprised by the entrance of such a figure as had never appeared before in that place. This was no other than a person habited in the exact uniform of an English jockey. His leathern cap, cut bob, fustian frock, flannel waistcoat, buff breeches, hunting-boots and whip, were sufficient of themselves to furnish out a phaeno-menon for the admiration of all Paris: but these peculiarities were rendered still more conspicuous by the behaviour of the man who owned them. When he crossed the threshold of the outward door, he produced such a sound from the smack of his whip, as equalled the explosion of an ordinary cohorn; and then broke forth into the hollow of a foxhunter, which he ut-tered with all its variations, in a strain of vociferation, that seemed to astonish and confound the whole assembly, to whom he introduced himself and his spaniel, by exclaiming in a tone something less melodious than the cry of mackarel or live cod, "By your leave, Gentlevolks, I hope there's no offence, in an honest plain Englishman's coming with money in his pocket, to taste a bit of your Vrench frigasee and ragooze."

Sir Stentor is here clearly a representative of a stock eighteenth-century comic type, of which Squire Western before him and Tony Lumpkin after-wards are obvious other examples. But his raw bumptiousness is counter-feit, and he turns out to be a consummate sharper. He strips Fathom of all his money and effects, and is later seen, "dressed in the most fashionable manner, and behaving with all the overstrained politesse of a native Frenchman."

Nearly all the English people in *Fathom* partake of one or the other aspect of Sir Stentor's character. They are credulous fools, the dupes of their own pretensions, like the fashionable folk in London to whom Fathom sells worthless jewels and antiques, or the set of people who credit him with profound medical knowledge, or else they are cunning villains, like Mr. and Mrs. Trapwell, or the attorney whom Fathom hires to defend him when he is sued by Trapwell, or Doctor Buffalo, the rich quack who effects Fathom's final ruin.

As the English people in *Fathom* are either fools or knaves, so the foreigners, within the "romance" sections of the novel, are virtuous nearly
without exception. What is more, the fact of their being foreign is frequently gratuitous in terms of the plot of the novel. After Fathom attempts
to rape Monimia, the heroine, she is rescued by Madame Clement, a
Frenchwoman living in London; the moral balance requires that Monimia's savior be, like herself, an alien in England. Similarly, the doctor who
tends Monimia throughout her illness, a minor character in terms of the
plot, is described as, "a humane man, and a foreigner," qualities that,
within the romance world of *Fathom*, are virtually synonymous. Madame
Clement is, "a humane gentlewoman"; the only man who will lend Renaldo the money he needs to travel to Vienna and claim his patrimony is
Joshua Manasseh, a Jew, and therefore, by English law at the time, an
alien. The officer who befriends Renaldo on his journey is an Irishman;
Renaldo himself is Hungarian, but his father, whose generosity had been
responsible for Fathom's advancement, "was originally of Scotland."
Monimia, *alias* Serafina, and her father, Don Diego, are Spaniards. The romance world, in which these characters move, is remarkably private and
self-contained. It has almost no contact with the society of England within
the framework of which it is placed, and it is therefore untouched by the
values of this society which form the chief concern of the "satiric" parts
of the novel. The social world of England is unworthy of Renaldo and
Monimia, a fact which is emphasized at the close of the novel when the
lovers have been married, and their return to material prosperity has been
achieved. Renaldo does not introduce his bride to his former acquaint-
ances, "because not one of them had formerly treated her with that delicacy of regard which he thought her due." As for Monimia:

> The fame of her beauty was immediately extended over this im-
> mense metropolis, and different schemes were concerted for
> bringing her into life. These, however, she resisted with unwea-
> ried obstinacy. Her happiness centred in Renaldo, and the cul-
> tivation of a few friends within the shade of domestic quiet.

As *Fathom* closes, Renaldo, Monimia, and Don Diego set sail for the Continent, Don Diego for Spain, and the others, "to reside in the Low Coun-
tries 'till his return." The romance characters have triumphed over Fathom
and the England which has provided so much scope for his talents. They
have lived in a private world of virtue and honor within the vicious and
dishonorable society around them, and having resisted the attempts of this
society to destroy them, they move away from it.

But Fathom's England, too, has its self-contained enclave of exiles, and we meet them in one of the greatest prison scenes in the eighteenth-century novel. As we might expect, most of the characters described are foreigners. The prison scene in *Fathom* is constructed around the historical figure of Theodore de Neuhoff, the former king of Corsica, who had been imprisoned in the King's Bench for debt in 1749. The story of de Neuhoff's life in England moves Smollett to reflect again on the English attitude toward strangers:

> The English of former days, alike renowned for generosity and valour, treated those hostile princes whose fate it was to wear their chains, with such delicacy of benevolence, as even dispelled the horrors of captivity; but, their posterity of this refined age, feel no compunction at seeing an unfortunate monarch, their former friend, ally and partizan, languish amidst the miseries of a loathsome gaol, for a paultry debt contracted in their own service.

Of the five members of Fathom's "club" within the prison, four are foreign. De Neuhoff himself was born in Metz, and his companions include Major Macleaver, an Irishman, Sir Mungo Barebones, a Scot, and an anonymous French chevalier. The fifth member, Captain Minikin, is, presumably, an Englishman. These characters are, of course, comic, as befits their place in the "satiric" portion of *Fathom*, but they are endowed with a certain dignity as well, and this places them apart from most of Smollett's caricatures. Sir Mungo Barebones, for example, the mad biblical scholar, is a brilliantly grotesque figure, but Smollett's description of him passes from the comic into the pathetic:

> Yet this figure, uncouth as it was, made his compliments to our adventurer in terms of the most elegant address, and in the course of conversation, disclosed a great fund of valuable knowledge. He had appeared in the great world, and bore divers offices of dignity and trust, with universal applause: his courage was undoubted, his morals were unimpeached, and his person held in great veneration and esteem; when his evil genius engaged him in the study of Hebrew, and the mysteries of the Jewish religion, which fairly disordered his brain, and rendered him incapable of managing his temporal affairs.

Within the context of comedy, the prison, like the expatriate world presided over by Madame Clement, is a place of humanity and honor. The king takes a kindly interest in Sir Mungo's lunatic scheme, and the duel by *assa foetida* fought between Major Macleaver and Captain Minikin, while grotesque, is fought out of a regard for female delicacy, and the result is accepted with good will. Unlike the free citizens of England, the inhabitants of the prison accept foreigners in a spirit of toleration. Captain Minikin says of the French chevalier, "the truth is, I believe his brain is a little disordered, and he being a stranger we overlook his extravagancies." The virtues of tolerance and humanity are liabilities in a society which rewards the corrupt, and those who possess these virtues are imprisoned for debt— they are failures, that is to say, in society's terms. Renaldo and Monimia reject the corrupt England depicted in *Fathom*, and are thus heroic, figures of romance. The inhabitants of the prison have lived and moved in this England, and must thus be figures of comedy, but they have failed, and are therefore endowed with a kind of heroism of their own.

The constant emphasis on the corrupt nature of society in England, which is demonstrated both directly in the actions of her citizens, and by contrast with the conduct of the foreign "romance" characters, furnishes *Fathom* with most of its satiric bite, but it also serves to deflate the grandeur of Fathom's villainy. The preface has prepared us for a confrontation between virtue and vice in the persons of Renaldo and Fathom, but England becomes the real villain of the novel, and this seriously weakens Fathom's effectiveness as a character. For an arch-fiend, designed by his creator to terrify readers away from the "irremediable gulph" of iniquity, dealing in cheap antiques and practicing medicine without the proper qualifications seem tame occupations, and Fathom's diabolism comes more and more to depend on his seductions. Ronald Paulson has pointed out that the five seductions or attempted seductions in the novel show Fathom in an increasingly villainous light as the women involved become progressively more innocent. But even here, as Paulson points out, Fathom succeeds only by playing upon the weaknesses of his victims, and the sense of outrage at his callousness is tempered by the reader's awareness of Elenor's vanity and Celinda's silly superstitiousness. Both stories are "pilot's charts" in Cleland's sense, and their function is not so much to mark Fathom's progress in degradation as to warn young ladies that men were deceivers ever. At the close of the Celinda episode, Smollett makes this quite explicit:

> This being the case, the reader will not wonder that a consummate traitor, like Fathom, should triumph over the virtue of an artless innocent young creature, whose passions he had entirely under his command. The gradations towards vice are almost imperceptible, and an experienced seducer can strew them with

such inticing and agreeable flowers, as will lead the young sin-
ner on insensibly, even to the most profligate stages of guilt. All
therefore that can be done by virtue, unassisted with experience, is to avoid every trial with such a formidable foe, by de-
clining and discouraging the first advances towards a particular
correspondence with perfidious man, howsoever agreeable it
may seem to be: for, here, is no security but in conscious
weakness.

The apogee of Fathom's wickedness is, of course, his attempt to seduce
Monimia, and this fails because she has no weaknesses for him to play
upon. He attempts to rape her, but is overawed by her courage, and gives
up his plot, having "lost no time in bewailing his miscarriage." Like Roderick Random and Peregrine Pickle, Fathom remains largely unchanged by
his adventures and by the various milieux in which they occur. All three
characters pass through a number of vicissitudes of fortune, and having
eventually come to understand the vanity of the world, all three withdraw
from it. The heroes of the earlier novels, having wed the heroines and
gained the birthrights out of which they had been cheated, move off to a
private rural paradise where they will live out the pastoral dream of country squirearchy, away from the snares and pitfalls of the world. Fathom,
too, is married, and proceeds to, "a cheap country in the north of England," where his penitence can be worked out in decent poverty and toil.
Renaldo and Monimia have never been part of the world through which
Roderick, Peregrine, and Fathom pass, their private paradise-world having
coexisted with the larger one, been threatened by it, and finally having
conquered it. They too, as we have seen, move away.

The spiritual regeneration of men through contact with a better world
than their own is the chief theme of *Humphry Clinker*, but it is also illustrated, perfunctorily, in *Fathom*. Both Don Diego and Fathom himself are
purged of their vices through contact with Monimia and Renaldo, and the
didactic effectiveness of the Richardsonian moral technique is therefore established; but this process does not involve any reconciliation between the
satiric and romantic aspects of the novel. The absolute separation of the
two worlds is insisted upon.

This separation of the two worlds of *Fathom* is emphasized, as we
might expect, in the style in which each is expressed. The characteristic
diction of the parts of the novel presided over by Fathom is ironic; in the
passages concerning the romantic adventures of Renaldo and Don Diego,
it is hyperbolical. The phrase "knight-errant," for example, is applied, obviously ironically, to Fathom and Ratchkali, to Sir Stentor Stiles and Sir

Giles Squirrel, the confidence men, and to Sir Mungo Barebones and the French chevalier; it is applied, seriously, to Renaldo during the fairytale adventure in which he rescues his mother from the tower where his wicked stepfather is keeping her prisoner. Here the term is used to underscore the nobility of Renaldo's actions, but its effect is hyperbolical in that it marks the movement of the plot into the romantic milieu of ladies imprisoned by ogres in towers. Smollett provides a real knight-errant in *Sir Launcelot Greaves*, and is forced to make him at least partially mad. The style of *Fathom* moves between the ironic and the romantic, and there is very little in between, precisely because the worlds these styles describe are mutually exclusive and irreconcilable. Irony and hyperbole are balanced at opposite ends of the scale of diction and are therefore appropriate for a novel as polarized in conception as *Fathom*. The principal ironic device employed is the mock-heroic, the mode with which the novel opens. Fathom's mother, the camp-follower, is compared with Semiramis, Tomyris, Zenobia, and Thalestris, while the infant Fathom himself, having been suckled on gin, "improved apace in the accomplishments of infancy; his beauty was conspicuous, and his vigour so uncommon, that he was with justice likened unto Hercules in the cradle." The scene in the King's Bench is mock-heroic in conception, rendered pathetic by the circumstance of the ex-king's historical fall from power. The duel by *assa foetida* within the prison is in the same tradition as the heroic games of the *Dunciad*. The mock-heroic functions ironically by emphasizing the contrast between pretension and action and thus deflating both. The style itself implies the standard by which the matter it describes is found wanting. The hyperbolic, romance style employed in *Fathom*, like the mock-heroic, is "high," its elevation serving to mark the contrast between its subject matter and the ordinary world of the day-to-day. It, too, implies a heroic standard, but its standard is fulfilled by the characters it describes. Out of the context of character, therefore, the styles are similar. Compare, for example, the following passages:

> "Light of my eyes, and empress of my soul! behold me prostrate at your feet, waiting with the most pious resignation, for that sentence from your lips, on which my future happiness and misery must altogether depend. Not with more reverence does the unhappy bashaw kiss the Sultan's letter that contains his doom, than I will submit to your fatal determination. Speak then, angelic sweetness! for, never, ah never will I rise from this suppliant posture, until I am encouraged to live and hope. No! if you refuse to smile upon my passion, here shall I breathe the last

sighs of a dispairing lover: here shall this faithful sword do the
last office to its unfortunate master, and shed the blood of the
truest heart that ever felt the cruel pangs of disappointed love."

"Can I then trust the evidence of sense? And art thou really to
my wish restored? Never, O never did thy beauty shine with
such bewitching grace, as that which now confounds and capti-
vates my view! sure there is something more than mortal in thy
looks! where hast thou lived? where borrowed this perfection?
whence art thou now descended? Oh! I am all amazement, joy
and fear! thou wilt not leave me! no! we must part again: by
this warm kiss! a thousand times more sweet than all the fra-
grance of the east! we never more will part. O this is rapture,
extasy, and what language can explain!"

The first of these passages is taken from Fathom's speech to the vain and
concupiscent jeweler's daughter, Wilhelmina, whose seduction he is about
to accomplish, while the second forms part of Renaldo's effusion upon
finding Monimia restored to him, as he thinks, from the grave. The style
of both passages is "high"; we readers never talk like this, even in our moments of passion, and the fact that Wilhelmina, unaware of this, is impressed by Fathom's words renders her a figure of comedy. We know what
Wilhelmina and Fathom are like, and the inappropriateness of such terms
as "angelic sweetness" to her and of such gestures as the threat of suicide
to him places the diction within the realm of the mock-heroic. The style
exposes its objects. The second passage is equally remote from the diction
of ordinary life, but here it is sincere. The fact that we do not talk like
Renaldo merely emphasizes the gulf between our world and his. Renaldo's
style is appropriate to his station; the novelist's problem is to give him a
character which will justify the style.

There is, to be sure, a difference between the two passages, even when
taken out of context. Fathom's speech, ornate as it is, is more prosaic than
Renaldo's, which is perpetually at the point of breaking into verse. Just as
the romance world in *Fathom* triumphs over the satiric world that surrounds and threatens it, so the true heroic style overcomes the mock-
heroic. Fathom's speech of penitence at the end of the novel is delivered in
a style indistinguishable from Renaldo's:

"Is there no mercy then for penitence! is there no pity due to
the miseries I suffered upon earth! save me, O bountiful heaven!
from the terrors of everlasting woe; hide me from these dreadful executioners, whose looks are torture: forgive me, generous

Castilian. O Renaldo! thou hadst once a tender heart. I dare not lift my eyes to Serafina! that pattern of human excellence who fell a victim to my atrocious guilt; yet, her aspect is all mildness and compassion. Ha! are not these the drops of pity? yes, they are tears of mercy: they fall like refreshing showers upon my drooping soul! ah murthered innocence! wilt thou not intercede for thy betrayer at the throne of grace!"

Fathom's world, the world of English society, has been conquered both in plot and diction, and the last view we have of this monster of ingratitude, covetousness, and lust shows him bathing the hand of Renaldo with tears. The novel thus ends with both its didactic intentions accomplished. The reader has been warned not to be duped by plausible confidence-men or deceived by artful seducers, and has been granted a vision of proper conduct embodied in the actions and sentiments of a worthy hero and heroine. *Fathom* belongs in the realm of comedy; it ends, fulfilling Byron's definition, with marriages all around, and it invokes the sense of new lives and fresh beginnings of which marriage is symbolic. But the effect of the novel, taken as a whole, is pessimistic. The bitterness behind it is intense, and while it is directed chiefly, as we have seen, at England and the English, it at times goes deeper than nationalism. The list of personal failings included in Smollett's ironic dedication of the novel to himself are evidence that he was under no illusion as to the perfection of his own character, while of the general race of men he tells us, in an authorial aside:

Success raised upon such a foundation [as a reputation for incompetence], would, by a disciple of Plato, and some modern moralists, be ascribed to the innate virtue and generosity of the human heart, which naturally espouses the cause that needs protection: but I, whose notions of human excellence are not quite so sublime, am apt to believe it is owing to that spirit of self-conceit and contradiction, which is, at least, as universal, if not as natural, as the moral sense so warmly contended for by those ideal philosophers.

If Fathom is not altogether right, "that the sons of men preyed upon one another, and such was the end and condition of their being," he is very nearly so, as the greater part of the novel makes clear. The pessimism implicit in this view ought structurally to be balanced by a final optimism engendered by the actions of the heroic characters, but the world of the heroic, as we have seen, is beleaguered in *Fathom*, and although it triumphs, it does not reform the world of the satiric but escapes from it.

The dualistic structure of *Fathom,* then, arises out of an attempt to reconcile the satiric adventure novel of the *Random-Pickle* type with the "higher" species of fiction, the chief practitioner of which was Richardson. This experiment takes the form of the creation of two protagonists, each of whom figures as the hero of a fictional world appropriate to one of these two novelistic types. The two worlds are sharply distinguished and are brought into conflict, but this conflict is finally divisive, and the separation of the ethoi of romance and satire is irreconcilable. Renaldo, Monimia, and Don Diego can change the character and destiny of Fathom, but from the society in which Fathom moved so freely they will remain foreign by virtue of the humanity which in the novel is often synonymous with foreignness. It is this irreconcilability which renders the effect of *Fathom* finally pessimistic. The duality of the novel is a formalistic experiment, but it is also a reflection of a dark and bitter view of human nature, a view in which the generous and good are outnumbered and besieged.

In Smollett's last and greatest novel, we again are shown characters at odds with society and with each other, but *Humphry Clinker* is a novel in which the process of regeneration is unifying rather than divisive. As if to emphasize that the pessimism of *Fathom* is not the last word, Smollett gives Fathom and Renaldo a place in *Humphry Clinker,* a place in which the process of regeneration is shown at work. In accordance with the novel's central metaphor of health, Fathom has become a healer, a country apothecary dedicated to the conscientious and disinterested service of the poor. By rescuing Renaldo and Monimia from an attack by highwaymen, Fathom both manifests his repentance and pays off the debt of gratitude which he owes, and the two worlds of *Fathom* are at last reconciled in the figure of the daughter of Fathom and Elenor, who is named after Monimia, and taken up by her.

But this is irrelevant to a study of *Fathom,* however neatly it completes and harmonizes that work, and the interest which the earlier novel holds for us must lie in its quality as a unique formal experiment, an experiment infused with bitterness, and enlivened by the hard, brilliant satiric style which is at once the projection and the justification of Smollett's spleen.

PHILIP STEVICK

Smollett's Picaresque Games

The critical apparatus used to examine picaresque fiction tends to carry us away from a consideration of the picaresque event. The word "episodic," for example, focuses critical attention upon structure; and it is ironically true that when one pays particular attention to episodic structure, one is apt to pay rather little attention to the episodes themselves; or the critic who analyzes the philosophical area indicated by such words as "determinism," "necessity," "choice," "chance," "fortune," "contingency," "luck" may illuminate the world view of picaresque fiction while running the risk of taking for granted the precise structure of those characteristic events upon which that world view is predicated. By using the word "picaresque" at all, we are naming a class of works by pointing to an agent; implicitly we are pointing to the acts the agent does, which we assume to show a remarkable consistency from work to work. We are handicapped by the difficulty of rendering "picaro" into English. If we call him a "rogue," then what he does is indulge in "roguery," a word so effete that it is incredible that it has survived as long as it has in discussions of picaresque fiction. If we speak of the picaresque event as a "trick" or "prank," we both narrow and trivialize it. One word which avoids a number of semantic pitfalls while opening certain fresh ways of looking at the picaresque event is the word "game." The word is neutral of value and allows for any degree of frivolity or intensity, any degree of structural simplicity or complexity, and it allows us to hold together in our minds the ideas

From *Tobias Smollett: Bicentennial Essays Presented to Lewis M. Knapp,* edited by G. S. Rousseau and P.-G. Boucé. © 1971 by Oxford University Press.

both of play and of the urgent relation to matters of survival which most picaresque events contain. It is, in fact, the special condition of picaresque fiction to have invested the game with all of the human tension which it can bear. Lazarillo de Tormes's indigent master, starving, picks his teeth. The picking of his teeth, in its social context, is a game. But there is no mistaking the fact that, as he is playing, he is really starving.

From our point of view in the twentieth century, Smollett appears to link the end of one tradition, the great tradition of classic picaresque, with the beginning of another tradition of related and derivative works, such as, in our century, *Felix Krull* and *Invisible Man*; and the common element of both groups, the one that leads up to Smollett and the one that leads away from him, is the interaction between a hero who is bright, quick, often naïve, and clever, and a society which is both powerful and cloddish, that interaction being a series of what we can loosely call games. Those interactions are at once endlessly various, inventive, surprising *and* limited, constricted, and predictable. Such is the nature of games in or out of books, that they be open to chance or excitement yet constrained by rules and "fields." We do homage to the variety of game in any picaresque work not only by speaking as easily as we do of its inventiveness but also by continuing to read a series of events so basically similar and so potentially monotonous. What we need to do, the variety being apprehensible, is to describe, on the other hand, the continuities of picaresque game, its basic paradigms, for in works so loosely organized it is in the repetitive nature of the game that we perceive the unity of the compositions. Smollett's pivotal position, at the end of the classic picaresque tradition, as translator of Lesage and assimilator of a wide range of earlier works, and as a precursor of the abrasive absurdities of the neo-picaresque that follows him, guarantees his ability to provide us with patterns of game not only peculiar to himself but suggestive of the nature of the genre.

Midway through *Roderick Random*, an epidemic of fever sweeps Roderick's ship. The climate is wretched, provisions are inadequate, and morale is low. The fever rages "with such violence, that three-fourths of those whom it invaded died in a deplorable manner; the colour of their skin being, by the extreme putrefaction of the juices, changed into that of soot." Roderick soon contracts the fever, suffers deeply yet manages to survive, largely because he has been able to take a berth apart from the ship's hospital, in which the absence of ventilation would virtually have ensured his death. During Roderick's illness he is visited by a friend, not by the ship's surgeon, who has no interest in him, and by the ship's parson, with whom he disputes doctrinal matters with such heat that his fever breaks and he is cured. Not knowing that he is suddenly much better, his friend Morgan returns to his side and, assuming him to be dead, groans, whines, and weeps, while Roderick, feigning death, stifles his own temptation to giggle. Morgan finally closes Roderick's eyes and mouth, "upon which I suddenly snapped at his fingers, and discomposed him so much, that he started back, turned pale as ashes, and stared like the picture of Horror. Although I could not help laughing at his appearance, I was concerned for his situation, and stretched out my hand, telling him I hoped to live and eat some salmagundy of his making in England." Recovered, Roderick uses his recovery as a reproach to Morgan, whose remedies did not cure him, to the ship's doctor, who in his indifference did not attend him, and to his rival, who had wished him dead. Implicitly, his recovery mocks the parson, who, in attempting to ease him into death, had cured him, and the captain, whose mindless neglect of the ship's hospital would have killed Roderick if he had not been able to subvert the captain's discipline.

The gulf that separates Roderick's game from such classic games as chess or such literary games as Holmes's outwitting of Moriarty is enormous. Take the question of choice, for example. Roderick does not self-consciously choose to dispute with the parson or to pretend, with Morgan, that he is dead in the way in which one "makes moves" in chess. There are no alternatives to anything he does, either in his own mind or in ours. There is no particular play of consequences, nor are there any rewards. Tricking Morgan is not, in any sense, winning, and had Morgan seen through his game, Roderick would not have lost. Roderick's game would be of no interest to the fashioners of those chaste mathematical formulae called game theory, which might not surprise us, but there is a basic sense in which Roderick's game would be incompatible also with the classic sociocultural theories of game, namely, those of Huizinga and Caillois, which should surprise us. For to Huizinga and Caillois, game, however central to culture, is defined nonetheless by its discrete separability from the useful and the serious, play being, by definition, gratuitous and nonserious; in Huizinga's word, "fun." In Roderick's game, the snapping at Morgan's fingers is inseparable from the almost dying, the exposure of the fraudulence of the ship's parson, the reality of the fever, the callousness of the captain, and so on. Unlike those moments in experience when we stop being productive and lay out the chess board, Roderick plays at the grimmest business life affords, staying alive in the face of substantial odds, and for him there is no separation between play and seriousness, no dialectic between them, but they are, in fact, identical.

Still, Caillois's categories of game can carry us toward a definition of the precise nature of Roderick's game, a game, or complex of games, representative of large areas of Smollett's fiction and central to Smollett's purposes. Caillois divides game into four types: *agon*, the contest (such as fencing or chess) in which the outcome depends upon superior strength, or tactic, or skill; *alea*, the game (such as dice or roulette) in which the decision is the result of chance; *mimicry*, the free improvisatory expression of the impulse to imitate; and *ilinx*, the pursuit of vertigo (as in skiing or auto racing), a deliberate attempt to confuse momentarily the stability of perception. We are accustomed, of course, to thinking of *agon* as the predominant form of picaresque game, in Smollett the perpetual result of humiliation and revenge, provocation and response, challenge and defense; the act of revenge or defense being a contest decided by superior cleverness. In the game I have cited, the *agon* is diffuse, with several antagonists, no clear conflict, and with a group of minor triumphs rather than a decision. Also elements of the other three games appear: Roderick's recovery depends heavily on chance, Caillois's *alea*, for example; and the entire action is performed under the disorientation of fever, suggesting Caillois's *ilinx*, a quality that can remind us of all the rolling eyes, the near swoons, and the drunken reeling about that accompanies so much action in Smollett. Taking for granted the fact, then, that every form in Smollett is apt to be diffuse and every category which one may reasonably apply to Smollett's fiction is apt to be cluttered by the simultaneous presence of a number of other categories, it is still possible to describe Roderick's game. It is as a combination of *agon* and *mimicry* that that game, and the typical game elsewhere in Smollett's picaresque fiction, can best be described; *mimicry* superimposed upon *agon*. The *agon* between Roderick and the captain, the doctor, and the parson is that classic picaresque struggle between the brighter, quicker, more clever picaro and institutional power. We know that Roderick, like every other picaro, will gain temporary victories but no substantial change. The captain will go on being tyrannical, the surgeon indifferent, and the parson full of casuistry. It is the triumph of Roderick to survive, *agon* by *agon*, against such institutional stupidity. But it is *not* enough, after all, to survive. In the act of surviving, which is, in itself, a game, Roderick plays at another game only tangentially related to survival. It is as if a chess player, in the act of winning a game of chess, were to occupy himself between moves by mugging, grimacing, and mocking the gestures of his opponent. If we remind ourselves, however, that Roderick's is no chess game but a grim business carried out in a cruel, repressive world in which no victory is more than temporary, the function of Roderick's *mimicry* becomes clear. Roderick plays his *agons* to stay alive; he mimics to *be* alive. And in the free invention of his *mimicry*, he transcends his cloddish antagonists, his limitations of choice, and his brutal world.

II

The shape of the picaresque event is determined to a large extent by its nature as a game. Or rather, in the case of Smollett, the shape of the event is determined by the somewhat discordant nature of its games, especially Smollett's peculiar combination of *agon* and *mimicry*. Of all of Caillois's categories, *agon* is apt to strike one as the most thoroughly circumscribed by rules. Any number of *agons*, for example, require a disinterested party, an umpire or a referee, for the express purpose of administering rules. Such *agons* as chess and fencing have vast protocols and elaborate lore accumulated around them. And even such crude agonistic confrontations as Indian wrestling still inevitably carry with them the obligation that they be conducted in some kind of mutually acceptable form. *Mimicry*, on the other hand, exhibits all of the characterstics shared by other forms of play, as Caillois points out, with one exception: that it is free of rules. It consists of incessant invention. Other pairs of Caillois's categories fit more easily and naturally together than do *agon* and *mimicry*, *agon* and *alea*, for example: it is easy to think of any number of games containing significant elements both of skill and chance. But *agon* and *mimicry* in certain ways pull the participant, and of course the writer as well, in opposite directions. And it is a special triumph of Smollett's art that he is able to reconcile the claims of two such different play impulses, the first tending toward symmetry, regularity, and ultimately, tedium, the other tending toward freedom, spontaneity, and, ultimately, incoherence.

The combination of the two is contained with particular purity in chapter 51 of *Peregrine Pickle*. Pickle and a certain Knight of Malta, having seen a performance of *Le Cid* by Corneille, argue over the comparative merits of the French and English stages.

> Our hero, like a good Englishman, made no scruple of giving the preference to the performers of his own country, who, he alleged, obeyed the genuine impulses of nature, in exhibiting the passions of the human mind; and entered so warmly into the spirit of their several parts, that they often fancied themselves the very heroes they represented; whereas the action of the Parisian players, even in their most interesting characters, was generally such an extravagance in voice and gesture, as is nowhere to be observed but on the stage. To illustrate this assertion, he availed himself of his talent, and mimicked the manner and voice of all the principal performers, male and female, belonging to the French comedy, to the admiration of the chevalier,

who, having complimented him upon this surprising modulation, begged leave to dissent in some particulars from the opinion he had avowed.

Presently the argument resumes, although the responses of Pickle tend to
be overwhelmed by the learning, the pseudo-learning, and the verbosity of
the knight. The *mimicry* of Pickle does not substantially alter the shape of
the event, which follows an agonistic logic of challenge and response; the
conventions of the *agon* are those of the debate, respect for evidence,
rhythm between the generalization and the supporting instance, certain
features of a public, oratorical rhetoric. But the position of the *mimicry*
allows it to dominate the event; and the values which the *mimicry* carries
alter every value that follows.

Those values can be roughed out with such words as "energy," "spontaneity," "élan"; unlike the learning of the knight, which is made to seem
self-congratulatory, pedantic, and quite forced, the *mimicry* of Pickle is
made to seem uncontrived and "natural." M. A. Goldberg has analyzed
Smollett's novels by positing a correspondence between their thematic
structure and the ideas of the Scottish common-sense philosophers. Certainly the antitheses which Goldberg finds—reason and passion, imagination and judgment, art and nature, social and self-love, primitivism and
progress—are at play in Smollett's works; and there is no doubt that such
antitheses are sufficiently stylized and intellectualized that it is defensible
to describe the novels' value structures with the aid of "ideas" found outside of the novels, in philosophy. But in Smollett's novels, like anybody
else's, there are values and values. What I mean by the values of the *mimicry* of Pickle as opposed to those of the pompous knight is a good deal
more sub-intellectual, or supra-intellectual, than the large thematic patterns which Goldberg finds with the aid of Scottish common sense. In the
long run, Pickle may come to be the embodiment, one may feel, of passion,
or imagination, or nature. In the short run, it doesn't matter. What does
matter is that he is alive.

More than his vitality, Pickle's *mimicry* has a dimension that draws
its power from the attribution to it of supernatural qualities. His *mimicry*,
that is, seems at once perfectly explainable and also magical. Smollett's
world is full of people who seem to be what they are not, but Pickle is one
person who can transform himself before our eyes into someone else without compromising his integrity of self. And although Smollett does not
render the mimicry with any amplitude, it is certainly his intention (note
the diction: "male and female," "admiration of the chevalier," "this sur-

prising modulation") to make Pickle's performance seem an extraordinary presentation, virtuoso, unaccountable, unique, and in its way magical.

Such *mimicry* as Pickle's, moreover, acts as the concrete representation of the picaro's nerviness, his cockiness, his colossal gall. Erving Goffman has chosen to take seriously the idea of "the action" as it is contained in that cant phrase "where the action is." "Action," as he defines it, "is to be found wherever the individual knowingly takes consequential chances perceived as avoidable." Given characters so imprudent as Roderick Random and Peregrine Pickle, every *agon* is *un*avoidable. They are bound to suffer humiliation, bound to burn for revenge, bound to be provoked, bound to fight. I have argued that their *mimicry* is a necessary mode of their continued self-assertion. But in any ordinary causal sense, their *mimicry*, unlike their *agons*, is avoidable, perceived as such by the reader and, insofar as we can infer their mental states, perceived as such by the characters. Their *mimicry* is a kind of chance-taking, always likely to expose them to additional hostility, always likely to fail in its effects, exposing them to still more ridicule. And the consequences of such *mimicry* may very well be, and often are, triumph and increased confidence, or, on the other hand, embarrassment, futility, a punch in the nose. The mimicry of Smollett's picaros is a splendid instance of Goffman's "action." And to see it as such is to see a linkage between Smollett's picaros and those driven characters of Goffman's essay, the gamblers, the hustlers, the vandals, the criminals, the professional athletes, the skydivers, the mountain climbers, for whom the events of routine experience are not enough and for whom the artificial production of an additional series of events with their own very real peril becomes a personal necessity.

Judged by the agonistic rules that govern the debate between Pickle and the chevalier, the latter wins, easily and decisively. But judged by the complex of values contained in Pickle's *mimicry*, the chevalier's victory is a hollow one. The *mimicry* is a small part of the total episode. But its function as a correlative for the high spirits of the hero and as a conveyor of those of his values which we are certainly expected to endorse make the *mimicry* far more important than its apparent prominence would lead us to believe. Not all *mimicry*, to be sure, is performed by Smollett's picaros. In chapter 46 of *Roderick Random*, for example, Roderick's new acquaintance Ranter mimicks Roderick's "air, features, and voice." Somewhat later, he makes an elaborate series of mock representations to Roderick's companion Wagtail, who becomes, as the chapter continues, the butt of several others' mimetic ingenuity. Roderick, throughout the chapter, is either victim or spectator, never the chief mime. Yet even though the personages change about, the values attached to certain actions remain substantially the same. People who play at identity are always distinct from people who assume a false identity for self-serving purposes. And the person who plays at identity is likely to be, however morally reprehensible, an interesting person, vital and alive.

Pickle and Pallet at one point in their travels approach Antwerp and the city, being the birthplace of Rubens, reminds Pallet of his idol.

> He swore . . . that he already considered himself a native of Antwerp, being so intimately acquainted with their so justly boasted citizen, from whom, at certain junctures, he could not help believing himself derived, because his own pencil adopted the manner of that great man with surprising facility, and his face wanted nothing but a pair of whiskers and a beard to exhibit the express image of the Fleming's countenance. He told them he was so proud of this resemblance, that, in order to render it more striking, he had, at one time of his life, resolved to keep his face sacred from the razor; and in that purpose had persevered, notwithstanding the continual reprehensions of Mrs. Pallet, who, being then with child, said, his aspect was so hideous, that she dreaded a miscarriage every hour, until she threatened, in plain terms, to dispute the sanity of his intellects, and apply to the chancellor for a committee.

Pallet's *mimicry* becomes the subject of the chapter. More is made of Pallet's imagined resemblance to Rubens. Ultimately he travels to the tomb of Rubens where he falls onto his knees in apparent adoration, to the considerable dismay of those at the church. Here is an example of *mimicry* which is patently ludicrous from start to finish. The most obvious reason that Pallet's *mimicry* is ludicrous is that he is no descendant of Rubens in any sense but is rather an unmitigated fraud, a terrible painter, and the butt of some of Smollett's coarsest humor. But the other reason is that he does not play. His *mimicry* is not his way of expressing his vitality, as it is with Roderick or Ranter; it is his pathetically serious way of seeking to express his own self-image, an assertion of appearance as if it represented essence. *Mimicry* which is not play comes close to the pathological.

The *mimicry* in Smollett's version of picaresque, then, is the chief conveyer of a complicated set of values; energy, vitality, quickness of invention, joy, and, more than all of these, a kind of personal stability, integrity, and authenticity. In a kind of fiction in which every character is more or less flat and every analysis is more or less perfunctory, the way we know who the characters are and the way we know that they have real human substance is through their modes of play. The bare structure, on the other hand, the rhythm and movement of the novel is provided by its successive *agons*. There are events in Smollett that are more or less pure *agon*, more or less pure *mimicry*, or neither, being perhaps melodramatic vignette without anything of the game about them. But ordinarily *mimicry* and *agon* interact in a fairly limited number of ways and these can first be set forth by returning to the pattern of Pickle's theatrical *mimicry*.

Pickle's theatrical *mimicry* precedes the main substance of the *agon*, and as the *agon* continues, Pickle does not return again to his *mimicry*. The *mimicry*, occurring at the beginning of the episode, provides Pickle with a means for "winning," at least in the eyes of the reader, for no amount of dialectical skill can really triumph over so splendid a mimetic talent. In the episode cited earlier, Roderick Random *mimics*, plays dead, at the end of the episode. He had already "won" against the captain, the parson, the disease itself, and his *mimicry* is a kind of triumphant foolishness, a parting shot not really at Morgan so much as at life itself. A third option allows Smollett to integrate the two, so that a character uses his *mimicry* as an agonistic tactic, playing back and forth between his strength and skill on the one hand and his mocking and posturing on the other. The use of *mimicry* at the beginning of an *agon*, as a kind of value base, the use of *mimicry* at the end of an *agon* as a self-defining gesture, and the integration of *mimicry* and *agon*, Stephen Potter fashion—these are the three basic structures of countless events in Smollett. And limited though these basic paradigms may be, individual instances are capable of demonstrating large dimensions of subtlety and considerable areas of aesthetic choice.

Chapter 45 of *Roderick Random* is rich and diverse enough to demonstrate a number of such choices. After the usual preliminary episodic business of settling into a location, Roderick goes to a playhouse "where I saw a good deal of company, and was vain enough to believe that I was observed with an uncommon degree of attention and applause." Imagining himself to be the center of so much admiration, Roderick

> rose and sat down, covered and uncovered my head twenty times between the acts; pulled out my watch, clapped it to my ear, wound it up, set it, gave it the hearing again; displayed my snuff-box, affected to take snuff, that I might have an opportunity of showing my brilliant, and wiped my nose with a perfumed handkerchief; then dangled my cane, and adjusted my

> sword-knot, and acted many more fooleries of the same kind,
> in hopes of obtaining the character of a pretty fellow, in the ac-
> quiring of which I found two considerable obstructions in my
> disposition, namely, a natural reserve, and jealous sensibility.

As a base for the play of values that is to follow, such *mimicry* is superb, showing, as it does, Roderick's vitality, his passionate wish to define and assert himself together with the gaucherie and the naïveté that makes it all ridiculous and, above all, the honesty toward himself, the insight into his own ridiculousness, the "natural reserve" that makes the passage rather touching to read, and, incidentally, one of the less picaresque events of the novel. As the play proceeds, Roderick is moved by the plight of the heroine and shares her tears, although he notices that no one else is similarly moved. And once again, Smollett has it both ways: Roderick's identifica-tion with the tragic situation on the stage is amusing and naïve; yet his susceptibility to the heroine's distress is very much related to his ability to mime—both depend upon an implicit *Einfühlung*, a rich responsiveness to the imagination of what it means to be someone else—and thus Roderick is not only more ridiculous, he is also more admirable, more interesting, more fully human than all of those facile and self-controlled popinjays who surround him in the boxes of the playhouse.

After the play is finished, Roderick encounters an attractive woman and persuades her to accompany him to a tavern. Roderick learns that she is a whore, but as he discovers this, he and the woman exchange tactic and move, precisely that kind of game I have described in which the agonistic structure is integrated with a continuing play of *mimicry*. The episode of the playhouse whore is followed by several pages of coffeehouse conversa-tion on that most typical of Smollett's subjects, the merits of the English versus the merits of the French. There is, throughout the conversation, much agonistic maneuvering, much bluster and pretense, much *mimicry*, although Roderick himself observes more than he participates. Ultimately the chapter works toward its last event, in which Roderick and an ac-quaintance argue over points of Latin grammar and diction, finally con-versing "a full two hours, on a variety of subjects" in Latin. In one sense, the ultimate *mimicry* consists of an utterly persuasive representation of an-other person. But in another quite legitimate sense, the ultimate *mimicry* consists of the sustained conversation (not merely schoolboy disputation) in another language, that language being the product of a culture detached from oneself by several centuries.

It is hard to imagine any system of analytical concepts being brought to bear on that chapter. It is harder still to imagine any critic who judges fiction according to its apparent structural control finding the chapter to be anything but a dismal failure, a sequence of some four main encounters without thematic unity and without even causal necessity. Yet it is a richly expressive chapter and is by no means so disunified as it may seem. For playing across every *agon* is an intermittent, quite unpredictable, but closely related series of *mimicries*, containing Roderick at the center and Roderick at the periphery, presenting Roderick, at the end of the chapter, as mimetic virtuoso and Roderick, at the beginning of the chapter, as mimetic fool. To see only the structure of the successive *agons* is to understand the chapter's events at their crudest level. To see *agon* and *mimicry* interrelated, on the other hand, is to understand the events as closely though not sequentially related vehicles for the arrogance and effrontery, the imagination and ingenuity, the energy and vitality, which is the particular source of power in Smollett's version of picaresque.

III

All picaresque novels show face-to-face relations with emphasis upon dissembling, fraud, disguise, and trickery. And to that extent all picaros are skilled mimes. Yet for Defoe's Roxana, to choose a contrast close to Smollett, such dissembling consists of assuming names not her own, wearing clothing that disguises her class or nationality or identity, suppressing her emotions, lying with a straight face. Nothing that she does, however, is comparable to the splendidly exuberant *mimicry* of Smollett's heroes. Smollett's picaros are not typical of their kind, and the difference lies, as A. A. Parker has pointed out, in the basic goodness of their impulses, a difference that has more than a little to do with their modes of play. "Good" and "bad" are not very relevant categories when applied to the worlds of *Lazarillo de Tormes* or *La Vida del buscón*. In an absolute sense, everybody is bad, the picaro among them. But in Smollett, however, fallible or even sometimes cruel his picaros may be, they are generally enraged by evil, compassionate toward the oppressed, honest in the long run if not the short, basically decent. Indeed, Parker maintains that *Roderick Random* is not picaresque at all since it is the world that is wicked in contrast to the hero, who is very far from that "delinquency" which Parker finds common to picaros within the European tradition.

Up to this point I have stressed the expressive value of *mimicry* in making concrete the vitality of Smollett's picaros. Insofar as they tend to be distinguishable from other picaros by their comparative goodness, it is appropriate to ask whether their *mimicry* is not merely a function of their vitality but also of their goodness. As a kind of coda to the present discussion, I wish to suggest that it is. Their games, taken together, contain examples of gratuitous malice, insignificant foolishness along with many *agons* in which their antagonists are unmistakably evil. The point is that even when their games are least ostensibly moral, we never forget that they are basically decent, capable of compassion and remorse. Above all, we never forget the controlling values of Smollett, who hated sham and exploitation with an uncompromising fierceness. Thus I mean to suggest that there is a special resonance in Smollett's picaresque games that is the result of the fact that they exist in relation to the implied limits of certain ethical imperatives.

Neither the historical richness of Huizinga's *Homo Ludens* nor the anthropological richness of Caillois's *Man, Play, and Games* suggests that play has had, and certainly had in the eighteenth century, an ethical dimension. In fact both Huizinga and Caillois, by stressing the gratuitousness of play, implicitly deny its ethical dimension. Caillois further discusses certain tendencies which overtake the play impulse, debasing it, and the idea of measuring play by ethical criteria would certainly be one such. Caillois is perfectly right: if we play because it is "good for us," we *are* debasing the play impulse. And Huizinga is also right: the extraordinary evidences of the play impulse in culture *haven't* anything to do with moral worth. Yet if we shift our perspective somewhat, we are easily enough persuaded that certain kinds of play are vicious and exploitative, hence "bad" or other forms of play are intolerably coarse, dehumanizing, in some other sense, "bad." What kind of games does a good man play? If we didn't think so anyhow, Smollett would demonstrate for us that the question is absurd, that almost any kind of play is possible without compromising one's basic goodness. Yet other fictional settings can as easily demonstrate that play has consequences that cannot finally be separated from the moral world in which it occurs: the manipulative and mendacious games in Samuel Butler's novels, for example, or those games in Evelyn Waugh's that succeed in trivializing the whole of life.

Hugo Rahner has undertaken a study of play, theological in its orientation, which begins by assembling a number of ancient valuations of play: Plato and Plotinus, Tertullian and Origen, Aristotle and Augustine, and above all Aquinas. What emerges from Rahner's study is a synthesis of certain pagan and Christian views of play in history and a remarkable meditation on God at play in the creative act. From the *Nicomachean Ethics* of Aristotle and later from early patristic writings, Rahner revives the ethical concept of "eutrapelia." The "eutrapelos," as Rahner summarizes Aristotle, is the man whose fondness for the playful exists in balance and harmony with his valuation for the serious. "This person," writes Rahner,

> stands between two extremes, the description of which is particularly important as showing how Aristotelian ethics emerged from the cult and politics of the city-state—a description which Aquinas later took over. The one extreme is the "bomolochos," the poor wretch who hung about the altar of sacrifice in the hope of snatching or begging an odd bit of meat; in a broader sense, one who was ready to make jokes at every turn for the sake of a good meal and himself to be made the butt of cheap gibes. The opposite extreme was the "agroikos," the "boor," whose coarse stiffness was despised by the "asteios," the highly cultured Athenian citizen.
>
> *(Man at Play)*

The means by which Rahner shows the transition of this Aristotelian grace and balance into Christian thought is less important for our purposes than the fact that such a transition does exist, that there is a long, impressive continuity in ethical thought, both Christian and non-Christian, which values play while recognizing the ethical perils in its excess.

Even if it could be demonstrated—which it cannot—that Smollett knew and loved the tenth book of the *Nicomachean Ethics*, that would not, I think, establish very much about the values of his fiction. Rahner's treatment does not at all provide the material for a possible "source." What it does provide is the idea that "eutrapelia," in one form or another, is a fairly constant virtue in ethical thought, that it is based so firmly in the cultural patterns of the West that it appears in philosophical writers of widely varying temperaments and world views. To put the matter another way, Rahner's treatment both codifies and confers great dignity upon an idea that is accessible to the common moral sensibilities of great numbers of people who have not read Aristotle and Aquinas. The general accessibility of the idea becomes especially apparent in the eighteenth century since the modes of play in the period are often highly developed and the introspective records of individual people in the period, their letters, journals, and private papers, tend often to be preserved and often to be extraordinarily honest and perceptive. There is scarcely a figure of consequence in literary eighteenth-century England who did not strive daily for "eutrapelia"; we are aware of the importance of the play impulse because it carries over into literature of the first rank more often than in other periods and we are aware of the efforts to keep such play impulses in balance because writers like Boswell tell us how difficult it is. And, as such writers in the eighteenth century make clear, striving for "eutrapelia" comes not merely out of social constraint but out of an implicit conviction of the union of play and ethics.

Of Smollett himself, no reader of the Noyes edition of the letters can fail to have been moved by the last letters in the collection. After the countless personal assaults and defenses, the literary wars, the ills real and imagined of the preceding pages, Smollett prepares to die and describes himself in a letter to Dr. John Hunter which is at once self-deprecatory and dignified, tough and affectionate, stoic and playful.

> With respect to myself, I have nothing to say, but that if I can prevail upon my wife to execute my last will, you shall receive my poor carcase in a box, after I am dead, to be placed among your rarities. I am already so dry and emaciated, that I may pass for an Egyptian mummy, without any other preparation than some pitch and painted linen.

The last letter of the collection is only a fragment, undated but evidently written before Smollett's daughter died in 1763.

> Many a time I do stop my task and betake me to a game of romps with Betty, while my wife looks on smiling and longing in her heart to join in the sport; then back to the cursed round of duty.

The easiest way to state the most widely held ethical ideal in the eighteenth century is to invoke the phrase that the eighteenth century often invoked itself, "to live well and to die well." The phrase can mean all things to all men, but to Smollett it meant the coexistence of wit and compassion, of "duty," as he puts it himself, and "romps."

Consider, then, the examples of *mimicry* I have cited as being characteristic of Smollett's picaros. In the first he tricks his best friend, who had thought him dead, but no sooner does he trick him than he is struck with remorse. Although it is proper for Roderick to celebrate his being alive and understandable that he should mock the muddle-headed solicitousness of Morgan, it all becomes, in the act, very close to vicious buffoonery: Roderick soothes the shock of Morgan the moment he has realized the impact of his *mimicry*. Pickle imitates the actors of the French stage in his disputation with the Knight of Malta not only out of high spirits, not only out of a sense of contest and a knowledge of his own mimetic talent, but out of an implied impulse toward balance in play. Roderick checks his own *mimicry* at the playhouse precisely out of his own insight that he has been excessive and foolish. As Smollett's picaros always know, although they do not say it, to play badly is to become distorted and grotesque, to join that gallery of living caricatures that forms the human background of the novels.

Pickle's first recorded act, at age nine months, is to contrive an alarming expression of mock pain, apparently for the malicious joy of seeing his elders try to relieve him of some nonexistent pin prick. His last recorded act is to spurn a visiting nobleman who had once behaved contemptuously toward him, by pretending that he is not Mr. Pickle at all. Despite his marriage and good fortune at the end no one would argue that he achieves "eutrapelia." There is scarcely a page of the novel (somewhat less so with Roderick Random), in which he is not boorish, coarse, or cruel. Yet it is also true that there is scarcely a page in either *Roderick Random* or *Peregrine Pickle* in which we are not aware of the judgment, either of Smollett or of the picaros themselves, that they are in danger of behaving boorishly, playing to excess. Of Pickle's infant mimicries, for example, we understand that he was treated with gratuitous cruelty in his infancy and that he has been surrounded by grotesques from his very birth; that he should play in a malicious manner is hardly surprising. Yet his games are "a peculiarity of disposition," described with ironic understatement at every point. And no one who reads of the anxiety that Smollett tells us his mock discomfort arouses in his mother is likely to find the infant Pickle's exploitation of her tenderness altogether amusing.

It would be a mistake, I think, to systematize the restraints that act upon the play of Smollett's picaros. Their guilt or embarrassment or remorse is always momentary, always highly specific; they improvise their moral response to experience. Smollett's narrative judgments of them are likely to be problematic, embedded in his rhetoric, every bit as *ad hoc* as their views of themselves, and just as unsystematic. The texture of Smollett's rhetoric, for example, is filled with man-beast images, which serve, among other things, to remind us of the sub-human possibilities that are always open to his human character, open, certainly, to his exuberantly mimetic picaros who are always in danger (to choose one of Smollett's own favorite beast metaphors) of becoming baboons. And the action of the novels is filled with reminders that the picaros, being skilled mimes, could lie, cheat, steal, and gamble so as to lay waste around them if they wished; but their play most often succeeds against the vain and the arrogant and they never become the vicious and indiscriminate confidence men which they have every native skill to become. In short, Smollett so constructed the characters of the picaros as to keep them in a perpetually unbalanced tension between their lust for game on the one hand and their moral constraint on the other.

Being comic characters set in the repetitive structure of episodic works, Smollett's picaros repeat certain paradigmatic events as the books proceed but they do not change. The unbalanced tension is never resolved. To the end, they are more aggressive than conciliatory. If we were ever persuaded that Roderick Random or Peregrine Pickle had achieved "eutrapelia," we would, I suspect, be disappointed. It is hard to imagine that their perfectly earnest wish for the good life, a life responsive to their own best judgment and their own sensitivity to the distress of others, should ever entirely temper their lust for *agon* and their delight in *mimicry*. They do not achieve "eutrapelia" not only because of the structure of the books in which they appear but because "eutrapelia" is a moral ideal difficult to attain. To play strenuously, ingeniously, and joyfully while keeping that play in a morally responsive balance with the whole of one's life, that is the possibility that lies behind Smollett's picaresque events. *Humphry Clinker* is, in a sense, a realization of such an ideal. But in the picaresque novels, "eutrapelia" is as difficult to achieve as Smollett knew it to be in actual experience.

THOMAS R. PRESTON

The "Stage Passions" and Smollett's Characterization

Arriving in London for the first time, Roderick Random and the faithful Strap attempt to dress in a manner befitting the capital. Strap's attire, in keeping with his friend-servant status, is less elegant than Roderick's but he does sport a "short crop-eared wig that very much resembled Scrub's in the play." This allusion to the eighteenth-century costuming of the servant in Farquhar's *Beaux' Stratagem* is merely one of numerous dramatic allusions running through Smollett's novels. The high incidence of such allusions recalls Smollett's own efforts as a playwright and indicates a lifelong fascination with dramaturgy and actual stage practice that makes him, as George Kahrl claims, "a rare example of the influence of the stage upon the novel." Such influence appears most obviously, perhaps, in the frequent tableaux-scenes that occur in the novels. This static arrangement or grouping of characters derives immediately from stage blocking and ultimately from the group composition of painting. The idea of dramatic scenes as "paintings expos'd upon the stage," to borrow a phrase from Dr. John Hill's *The Actor* (1750), underlies the famous definition of the novel Smollett supplies in the preface to *Ferdinand Count Fathom*. Smollett argues that the "novel is a large diffused picture, comprehending the characters of life, disposed in different groups and exhibited in various attitudes, for the purposes of an uniform plan." To fulfill this plan, however, the novel also needs a "principal personage" who will "attract the attention, unite the incidents, unwind the clue of the labyrinth, and at last close the

From *Studies in Philology* 71, no. 1 (January 1974). © 1974 by University of North Carolina Press.

scene, by virtue of his own importance." As the terms "close the scene" suggest, Smollett associates the "principal personage" with those heroes "who have hitherto succeeded on the English stage."

While the stage undoubtedly influenced the tableaux-structure of many scenes in Smollett's novels, it even more significantly, I think, shaped his method of characterization. Albrecht Strauss points out in an excellent study that Smollett relies almost completely on external physical reaction to depict the internal emotional states of his characters. Using the reunion of Serafina and Don Diego in *Count Fathom* as exemplary of Smollett's approach, Strauss notes that the scene calls for the expression of "Don Diego's mingled feelings of relief, incredulity, fondness, gratitude, and shock." Smollett's depiction of this complex of emotions seems woefully deficient.

> This powerful shock aroused his faculties; a cold sweat bedewed his forehead; his knees began to totter; he dropped upon the floor, and throwing his arms around her, cried, "o nature! O Serafina! Merciful Providence! Thy ways are past finding out." So saying, he fell upon her neck, and wept aloud.

Here are certainly no "subtle Jamesian analyses of states of feeling." Smollett focuses instead on biological and bodily reactions, directing attention to Don Diego's sweaty forehead, tottering knees, collapse to the floor, frantic embrace, stylized cries to heaven, and weeping. But this whole physiological melange and Smollett's method of characterizing in general take on a new meaning when we recall with Kahrl that Smollett "consciously proposes to employ in prose-fiction the methods and purposes of the drama in character portrayal." Smollett's characterization depends on the "stage passions" and assumes at least a nodding acquaintance with the acting theory of the era.

I

The methods and purposes of eighteenth-century drama in character portrayal were not based on any theory of internal analyses. They derived instead, as Brewster Rogerson points out, from the theory that the passions were to be represented in art by "outward visible or audible signs." Aristotle, Rogerson points out, claimed that the passions are changes in the soul revealing "themselves in distinguishable outward signs—in characteristic gestures, sounds, and facial alterations." Classical writers, especially Aristotle and Quintilian, either implied or stated that "it should be possible to reproduce any of the major human affections simply by making a faithful copy of the outward signs." Based on apparent classical precedent, French neoclassical critics developed the theory of "painting the passions" and sought to arrive at a "comprehensive system of affective norms, " or more simply a "grammar of the passions." The French Academy of Painting and Sculpture devoted more than forty years to compiling rules for representing the passions, and Charles Le Brun's *Expression des passions,* influencing even Jonathan Richardson and Hogarth, became a kind of illustrated bible of the major passions. "In every art of their day," Rogerson points out, "and not merely in painting, it was the special praise of a good workman and a wise student of human nature that he knew how (as the phrase went) to paint the passions in their general truth." The theory of painting the passions was as prevalent in England as in France, and there it affected no art, perhaps, more than the art of acting, forming the underlying theory of the various schools of acting then on the stage.

Central to the acting theories was the idea that an actor must be *natural.* This idea and the assumption that the art of acting is based on the theory of painting the passions are endorsed in Smollett's *Peregrine Pickle.* Debating with the Knight of Malta about French and English styles of acting, Perry offers the following defence of English acting:

> Our hero, like a good Englishman, made no scruple of giving the preference to the performers of his own country, who, he alleged, obeyed the genuine impulses of nature, in exhibiting the passions of the human mind; and entered so warmly into the spirit of their several parts, that they often fancied themselves the very heroes they represented.

Perry's praise of English acting is followed by the Knight of Malta's famous attack on what he considers Garrick's failure to paint the passions accurately, an attack Smollett changed in the second edition of the novel to a brief compliment. The compliment offered in the second version more truly reflected the sentiment of the era, for Garrick served as the living symbol of the *natural* actor accurately painting the passions.

Arthur Murphy argues in the *Life of David Garrick* (1801) that when the fledgling actor took the stage "the drama was sunk to the lowest ebb; in tragedy, declamation roared in a most unnatural strain; rant was passion; whining was grief; vociferation was terror, and drawling accents were the voice of love." Garrick sought to be a *natural* actor, and "shone forth like a theatrical Newton," according to Thomas Davies; "he threw new light on elocution and action; he banished ranting, bombast, and grimace; and restored nature, ease, simplicity, and genuine humour." As a *natural* actor Garrick possessed the ability to feel his role. Murphy writes,

"He was sensibly alive to all the passions, and acted from the impulse of his feelings; his heart was his prompter, and under that guide, he was sure to imitate nature." Feeling his role, however, was not enough, for Garrick made it a point to understand intellectually everything he could about the passions.

> The passions, and all their operations, were his constant study; their turns, and counterturns, their flux and reflux, and all their various conflicts, were perfectly known to him; he marked the celerity with which they rise and shift; how they often blend, unite, and raise one mixed emotion, till all within is in a state of insurrection.

Presumably his knowledge of the passions and his ability to feel them allowed Garrick to represent them externally with such brilliance. As Thomas Wilkes noted, "His knowledge of the passions, and their several methods of operating on the mind, are by him through the whole very properly marked."

Garrick's acting methods followed the theories, for the schools of acting and the theatrical critics all agreed that the actor must imitate nature, that he must be *natural* in whatever character he portrayed. The appeal to nature meant, in effect, that the actor must feel his role. As Robert Lloyd enjoins in *The Actor* (1760), "To this one Standard make your just Appeal / Here lies the golden Secret; learn to *feel*." If the actor "does not himself feel the several emotions he is to express," claims John Hill, he "will give but a lifeless and insipid representation of them." The concept of feeling the role went very deep, implying the modern sense of losing the self in the character. In *A General View of the Stage* Thomas Wilkes makes the meaning of feeling the role unequivocally clear. "To do justice to his character," argues Wilkes, the actor "must not only strongly impress it on his mind, but make a temporary renunciation of himself and all his connections in common life, and for a few hours consign all his private joys and griefs to oblivion; forget, if possible, his own identity." The truly *natural* actor must then emotionally identify with or become the character he impersonates on stage.

To feel the role as deeply as he should, the actor, as Garrick had done, was enjoined to comprehend intellectually all the various passions of human nature. As that indefatigable commentator on acting, Aaron Hill, writes in his *Essay on the Art of Acting* (1746), "To act a passion well, the actor must never attempt its imitation, 'till his fancy has conceived so strong an image, or idea, of it, as to move the same impressive springs within his mind, which form that passion, when 'tis undesigned, and natural." Hill's terms "to act a passion" clearly suggest that acting is based on the theory of painting the passions, in fact, to borrow Wilkes's language, that "The Theatre, whether viewed in a tragic or comic light, is a lively picture of the human passions." In painting this picture, the actor was supposed to be representing the various passions or internal emotional states through his external gesture, tone of voice, pronunciation, bodily movement, and facial expression. Garrick himself understood the theory he exemplified on the stage. He writes:

> Acting is an *Entertainment of the Stage*, which by calling in the Aid and Assistance of *Articulation, Corporeal Motion*, and *Ocular Expression, imitates, assumes*, or *puts on* the various *mental* and *bodily Emotions* arising from the various Humours, Virtues and Vices, incident to human Nature.

Putting on the various mental and bodily emotions clearly meant putting on characteristic outward signs. "An Actor," Aaron Hill points out, "is the professor of an art that represents, to the eyes and ears of an audience, the whole diversity of passions, whereby human life is distinguished throughout all its conditions, whether of good or bad fortune." If these passions are to be represented, however, the actor must possess a "knowledge of those passions and a power to put on, at will, the marks and colours which distinguish them."

As the last quotation from Aaron Hill suggests, learning the passions emotionally and intellectually implied that there were specific outward signs or marks distinguishing the passions—a grammar of the passions. Smollett vividly illustrates the idea of a grammar of the passions in *Roderick Random*. During the scene portraying the reunion of Roderick and Strap in France, Smollett reduces Strap's various emotional responses to Roderick's adventures into a catalogue of supposedly characteristic external marks.

> During the recital, my friend was strongly affected, according to the various situations described. He *started* with surprise, *glowed* with indignation, *gaped* with curiosity, *smiled* with pleasure, *trembled* with fear, and *wept* with sorrow, as the vicissitudes of my life inspired these different passions [italics mine].

This scene provides, in effect, the basics of a grammar for expressing externally the passions of surprise, indignation, curiosity, pleasure, fear, and sorrow.

Such a short-cut way of expressing Strap's successive emotional states merely translates acting theory into fictional characterization. As the classical writers noted by Rogerson implied, the passions evoked external marks that were characteristic, and since they were characteristic they were also *natural*. "The signs which we use to express these several intentions of the soul," argues John Hill, "are not however merely arbitrary; they are dictated by nature's self, and are common to all mankind." Invoking classical precedent, Wilkes writes, " 'Nature,' as Cicero observes, 'has assigned to each passion and sentiment its peculiar air of countenance and gesture.' " In the *Prompter* Aaron Hill provides the kind of "physiological" rationale that lay behind the grammar of the passions.

> Every passion has its peculiar and appropriate look, and every look enforces an adapted and particular tone in the sound of the voice and a consequent and necessary action in the modification of the body, because when the heart has communicated its sensation to the eye, every muscle and dependent nerve, catching impulse in a moment, must concur to assist the impression, whence, as no action can be proper but one that paints an idea, so, no look can be excusable but that which is the result of intention.

So focused was the grammar of the passions on the external signs of bodily movement and gesture that it was possible for John Hill to suggest that speech was not absolutely necessary for painting the passions. "Without the assistance of words," he claims, "we are able to signify by gestures and signs our hopes, our fears, our satisfaction, or our displeasure."

Smollett repeats Hill's idea in *Peregrine Pickle* when one of the "playhouse censors," praising Quin, claims, "Over and above the distinctness of pronunciation, the dignity of attitude, and expression of face, his gestures are so just and significant, that a man, though utterly bereft of the sense of hearing, might, by seeing him only, understand the meaning of every word he speaks!" Perry objects that Quin's painting of the passions is really so exaggerated that it fails to represent them accurately: "Were the player debarred the use of speech, and obliged to act to the eyes only of the audience, this mimicry might be a necessary conveyance of his meaning; but when he is at liberty to signify his ideas by language, nothing can be more trivial, forced, unnatural, and antic, than this superfluous mummery." Perry is not denying the need to paint the passions, but rather arguing that their representation must be *natural* or characteristic, as he later explains.

Not that I would exclude from the representation the graces of action, without which the choicest sentiments, clothed in the most exquisite expression, would appear unanimated and insipid; but these are as different from this ridiculous burlesque, as is the demeanour of a Tully in the rostrum, from the tricks of a Jackpudding on a mountebank's stage. And, for the truth of what I allege, I appeal to the observation of any person who has considered the elegance of attitude and propriety of gesture, as they are universally acknowledged in the real characters of life.

Behind Perry's objection probably lies John Hill's contention that "The paintings expos'd upon the stage, are seen at a certain distance by the greater number of the audience: they must therefore have a strength in the touches somewhat too bold for a near view; but yet so moderated, that it may be overlooked by those who have that situation, in consideration of the necessities of the rest." In any event, it seems clear that when Smollett depicts the emotional states of his characters through external, bodily reactions, he is following the dominant acting theories of his day—he is attempting to paint the passions according to a supposedly "natural" grammar of external marks.

II

Despite the repeated insistence that the actor must know and feel the passions he paints, the equally repeated insistence that every passion possessed its external marks implies that these marks can be organized into rules the actor can learn, whether or not he knows and feels the passions they supposedly represent. Thomas Wilkes claimed that a complete grammar of the passions could probably not be given: "As this art is so extensive, and admits so much variety of improvement, it cannot be expected that a complete system of rules should be immediately advanced." Nevertheless both Wilkes and Aaron Hill attempt a rather thorough grammar, and all of the theatrical critics discuss the marks of the major passions, usually with copious illustration. Underlying the rules of the grammar were two general principles: in representing a passion both the degrees of its intensity and its decorum should be observed. By *decorum* the critics meant the different representation of the same passion according to such diverse criteria as social status, age, occupation. But it could also mean the more difficult problem of distinguishing the same passion in comedy and tragedy. Using, for instance, Macbeth's terror at the murder of Duncan and Abel Drugger's terror at the breaking of a urinal in *The Alchemist* as examples, David Garrick complains:

> If an Actor . . . in assuming these different Characters with the *same Passions,* shall unskilfully differ only in *Dress,* and not in *Execution;* and supposing him right in *One,* and of Consequence absolutely ridiculous in the *Other.* Shall this Actor, I say, in Spite of Reason, Physicks, and *common Observation,* be caress'd, applauded, admir'd? But to illustrate it more by Example.—Suppose the *Murder of Duncan,* and the *Breaking* a *Urinal* shall affect the Player in the same Manner, and the only Difference is the *blue Apron* and *lac'd Coat,* shall we be chill'd at the *Murderer,* and *roar* at the *Tobacconist?*

Garrick obviously expects comic and tragic terror to be differently represented, but as we will see below, he offers no external marks that clearly distinguish the two. Like Garrick, Smollett also distinguishes between comic and tragic decorum and extends decorum to cover even nationality. In his debate with the Knight of Malta, Peregrine Pickle asserts: "The player in question [Garrick] . . . has, in your opinion, considerable share of merit in the characters of comic life; and as to the manners of the grand passions of the soul, I apprehend they may be variously represented, according to the various complexion and cultivation of different men. A Spaniard, for example, though impelled by the same passion, will express it very differently from a Frenchman."

Despite his allegiance to the ideas of *natural* acting and of passional decorum, when depicting the emotional states of his own fictional characters, Smollett inevitably employs what can only be called a formulaic approach to characterization. As Strauss argues, there "is a tendency to lapse into ready-made formulas whenever the occasion for describing strong emotions arises. Whether the emotion be rapture or distress, anger or terror, Smollett always has a readily available repertoire of descriptive phrases to fall back upon. To adapt these to a particular situation all he needs to do is to rearrange or embroider." Whenever Smollett wishes to depict the passion of fear, for example, he merely varies a formula whose basic elements can be seen "in an account of Davy Dawdle's terror in *Sir Launcelot Greaves*: 'His hair bristled up, his teeth chattered, and his knees knocked.' " Almost the same terms are used to describe Fathom's fear when he discovers himself locked in a room with a dead body: "Then his heart began to palpitate, his hair to bristle up, and his knees to totter."

Smollett's formulaic approach followed logically from the grammar of the passions. Thomas Wilkes claimed that the various rules in the grammar of the passions he offered the actor were "only intended to be an useful hint, and assistant to his genius, but not to fetter or confine it." In fact, however, the rules served precisely as fetters, for they obscured the idea that the external marks were supposed to be "natural" and instead articulated formulas to represent the passions. The tendency to formula can be readily seen in the rules for representing fear given by Aaron Hill, Wilkes, and Garrick. Each set of rules varies slightly, but each establishes a pattern of movement the actor can commit to memory and follow at will. Aaron Hill describes the dynamics of making the transition from grief to fear.

> if he would strike out, in an instant, the distinction, by which fear is diversified from sorrow, let him only, in place of that re-sign'd, plaintive, passive, distress, that is proper to *grief*, add (without altering the relax'd state of his nerves) a starting ap-prehensive, and listning [sic] alarm to his look; keeping his eyes widely stretch'd, but unfix'd; his mouth still, and open; his steps light and shifting,—yet, his joints unbrac'd, faint, nerveless.

Wilkes's rules for expressing fear are basically the same as Hill's, but more generalized:

> The apprehension of an approaching evil, or of being deprived of our happiness in any shape, creates fear: its symptoms are a pale countenance, a troubled eye, a depression of the spirits approaching to fainting: when it rises to terror or horror, a tremor and universal agony follow; the speech is broken and confused, and the half formed accents die upon the lips.

Garrick's rules attempt to describe comic as opposed to tragic fear. Using the urinal as his example, Garrick sets down rules that are so specific they provide an exact model for the actor to copy.

> How are the different Members of the Body to be agitated? Why Thus,—His *Eyes* must be revers'd from the object he is most intimidated with, and by dropping his *Lip* at the same Time *to* the Object, it throws a trembling *Languor* upon every *Muscle*, and by declining the right Part of the Head towards the *Urinal*, it casts the most *comic Terror* and *Shame* over all the *upper* Part of the Body, that can be imagin'd; and to make the *lower* Part equally Ridiculous, his *Toes* must be *inverted* from the *Heel*, and by holding his *Breath*, he will unavoidably give

> himself a *Tremor* in the *Knees,* and if his *Fingers,* at the same
> Time, seem convuls'd, it finishes the compleatest low picture of
> *Grotesque Terror* that can be imagin'd by a *Dutch Painter.*

Garrick thinks that this description clearly distinguishes comic from tragic
fear, and yet it is by no means clear how the bodily movements he gives
Drugger differ greatly from these Aaron Hill ascribes to the representation
of fear in general. It is essentially the same formulaic approach made even
more detailed.

If the rules actually adumbrated formulas for representing the passions, nearly every formula, paradoxically, could also be used to represent
almost any passion. This paradox, I think, accounts for another important
aspect of Smollett's characterization, his tendency to apply the same formula indiscriminately to different passions. Smollett's depiction of
Fathom's fear, for example, included tottering knees; this, however, is the
same formula used to render Don Diego's surprise and joy at finding his
daughter, Serafina. Perry's jealousy is brought out by the description "the
sweat ran down his forehead in a stream, the color vanished from his
cheeks, his knees began to totter, and his eyesight to fail." The tottering
knees appear again, but now as a physical manifestation of jealousy, and
they reappear, along with sweat and bristling hair, to describe Trunnion's
terror: "a cold sweat bedewed his limbs, his knees knocked together, his
hair bristled up, and the remains of his teeth were shattered to pieces in
the convulsive vibrations of his jaws." This same "cold sweat" described
Don Diego's joy, while, in a milder form, the teeth "business" and the loss
of facial color describe Matt Bramble's anger: "his eyes began to glisten,
his face grew pale, and his teeth chattered." The application of formulas,
even indiscriminately, works brilliantly when the scene is focused on the
comically grotesque qualities of Smollett's celebrated "originals." But for
a serious differentiation of emotional states, the indiscriminate application
of formulas fails, for the formula alone does not tell the reader just what
emotion the character is experiencing. Foote's comment about the actor
Spranger Barry is to the point. Barry's "Expressions of Grief and Tenderness are very becoming," Foote claims, but he runs a great risk of blurring
passional differences, for his "hackneying the Passion, and applying it indiscriminately, will take from its Weight, and lower its Force. . . . If you
cry one Minute for Joy, and another for Sorrow, as in Lord *Townly,* a
Man would be puzzled to know whether you were angry or pleased."

Smollett's fictional characters inherit the formulaic paradox that external physical manifestations, while referring to different passions, may
still exhibit themselves identically. The theatrical critics are often, indeed,
reduced to suggesting that only in the eye, ironically that part of the anat-

omy perhaps least visible to an audience, can the different passions be completely marked. Aaron Hill calls the eye the "show-glass of the soul," and Thomas Wilkes argues "that all these Passions are more or less distinguishable in the eye: Joy, Love, and grief, are seen in an animated or cloudy look." Aaron Hill ultimately makes the eye the only truly distinguishing external mark of different passions: "Unless an actor has accustomed his reflection to examine distinctions in passion, he will be surprized, to be told, in this place, that there is no other difference but the turn of an eye, in the expression of *hatred* and *pity*." This emphasis on the eye probably explains Smollett's frequent use of eye movement in his passional formulas. One depiction of fear in *Roderick Random,* for example, includes the phrase "his eyes staring"; Roderick's joy at being reunited with Narcissa evokes cloudy eyes: "a sudden mist overspread my eyes!"; frightened at Sir Launcelot Greaves, Ferret's "eyes retired within their sockets"; Bramble's anger at Colonel Rigworm is rendered in part by the phrase "his eyes began to glisten." References to the eye in the formulas, however, do not resolve the paradox that different passions may still evoke identical physical reactions.

Since both Aaron Hill and Wilkes offer the most comprehensive grammar of the passions, their repeated references to the similarity of the rules make the paradox stand out clearly. Hill begins to describe the transition from grief to fear by noting: "Here, an actor, who would impress his imagination with a natural idea of fear, will most effectually represent it, by assuming the same languor, in look, and in muscles, that was, just now, described, as peculiar to *grief*." Although he does not admit it, Hill has, in effect, destroyed the very idea that a passion evokes natural marks that will effectively represent and distinguish it. Hill, in fact, seems to rejoice in his later announcement that the external marks of joy and anger closely resemble each other.

> Few would imagine, that the lineaments of *joy* and *anger* should unite in any point of strong resemblance! And yet, 'tis evident, they only differ in a change of look: For, as to the intensely bracing up the nerves, *that* is the same, exactly, in both passions, and the sole distinction lies in this:—a *smile* upon the eye, in bodies strongly braced, compels the voice to sound of joy—while *frowns,* in the same eye (without the smallest alteration of the muscles) immediately transform the gay sound, to a dreadful one.

Without the distinguishing mark of the eye, the external, physical manifestations of joy and anger are exactly the same.

The rationale for Smollett's application of formulas indiscriminately becomes startlingly clear when Wilkes's rules for fear, anger, and rage are compared. For Wilkes the marks of fear are "a pale countenance, a troubled eye, a depression of the spirits approaching to fainting"; when fear becomes terror "a tremor and universal agony follow; the speech is broken and confused, and the half formed accents die upon the lips." The marks of anger have a few added details, but a close resemblance exists: "Anger runs through the mind like a devouring flame; it choaks the voice, gives a savage wildness to the eye; the eyebrow in this disposition is let down, it is contracted, and pursed into frowns. This passion will sometimes excite a trembling in the whole frame." Anger and rage, however, can hardly be distinguished: "when rage inflames the mind, the eye kindles, and the whole frame is agitated." Any one of these rules could have inspired what Strauss calls Smollett's basic formula for fear: "His hair bristled up, his teeth chattered, and his knees knocked." And the basic formula for fear can, in terms of the grammar of the passions, just as well represent anger, rage, and, from Aaron Hill's perspective, almost any passion. At the end of his *Essay,* Hill supplies an abbreviated version of the rules for representing the ten major passions, and except for the look in the eye, six of the rules are identical. They deserve listing to show how the rules for representing a particular passion inevitably led to their application to nearly all passions indiscriminately.

> Joy is expressed by muscles intense—and a smile in the eye.
> Anger, by muscles intense—and a frown in the eye.
> Pity, by muscles intense—and a sadness in the eye.
> Hatred, by muscles intense—and aversion in the eye.
> Wonder, by muscles intense—and an awful alarm in the eye.
> Love, by muscles intense—and a respectful attachment in the eye.

III

When viewed against the background of eighteenth-century acting theory, Smollett's use of external, bodily reactions to depict the internal emotional states of his characters, the formulas into which these external reactions fall, and their application to almost any passion indiscriminately become much more comprehensible. Understanding this background does not, of course, convert Smollett's characters into introspective, Jamesian individuals. But it does suggest that Smollett must be read for different virtues. The "stage passions" of his characters point, for one thing, to the importance of character in action. The depiction of internal emotional states through external physical marks tend to present the individual in terms of a context of significant relationships. The individual undoubtedly enjoys unique emotional states, but that is only part of the story. He also exists in relationship to other individuals, institutions, and society. And, to borrow Heidegger's concept of human *Dasein*, these unique emotional states cannot ultimately be defined except within the context of those significant relationships. As Kurt F. Reinhardt, commenting on Heidegger, observes, "Man, as existing, is actively related to the objects and beings which surround him, and without his active insertion into the world knowledge would be impossible. If man tries to withdraw himself from the world in detached observation, he perceives only the external aspects of things but fails to penetrate into their essential meaning. To seize reality man must live and act." The technique of using the "stage passions" allows Smollett to dwell on the dynamics of an individual's interaction with a context, and this context is as important as the individual. In fact, Smollett's application of formulas indiscriminately forces one to understand the context in order to understand the precise meaning of the passions the formulas supposedly represent.

This evaluation of Smollett's "stage passions" can be illustrated by a close examination of almost any scene in the novels. When Roderick Random, for example, sees Narcissa for the first time after their long separation, his emotional response is described in typical passional formulas.

> a gentleman dressed in a green frock came in, leading a young lady, whom I immediately discerned to be the adorable Narcissa! Good Heaven! what were the thrillings of my soul at that instant! my reflection was overwhelmed with a torrent of agitation! my heart throbbed with surprising violence! a sudden mist overspread my eyes! my ears were invaded with a dreadful sound! I paused for want of breath, and, in short, was for some moments entranced!

Roderick is, of course, trying to express his surprise, joy, and sexual excitement, but, if taken out of context, this description of his internal emotions could just as well refer to hate, fear, or rage. The terms "adorable Narcissa" are the clue to Roderick's internal emotional state; Smollett's real concern, however, is with the interpretation of that state in terms of its context of significant relationships. In the first place, Roderick's emotional response to Narcissa is ironically juxtaposed to his current and ignoble quest for a wealthy heiress. The reunion with Narcissa occurs at a ball, and her appearance immediately follows a passage describing Roderick's delight at receiving permission to escort, without her mother, Miss Snapper, his latest matrimonial prey.

> Next day I put on my gayest apparel, and went to drink tea at Mrs. Snapper's according to appointment, when I found, to my inexpressible satisfaction, that she was laid up with the toothache, and that Miss was to be intrusted to my care.

Roderick's joy at seeing Narcissa relates back to his fortune-hunting courtship of Miss Snapper, and at the same time it points forward to his ill-treatment of Miss Snapper during the course of the ball. Straining to keep Narcissa in his view, Roderick pauses to comment on his neglect of Miss Snapper.

> it may easily be imagined how ill I entertained Miss Snapper, on whom I could not now turn my eyes without making comparisons very little to her advantage. It was not even in my power to return distinct answers to the questions she asked from time to time, so that she could not help observing my absence of mind; and, having a turn for observation, watched my glances, and, tracing them to the divine object, discovered the cause of my disorder.

Even Roderick's knowledge of Miss Snapper's discomfort fails to reassert in him the "gentlemanly" qualities he prizes so highly.

> At any other time, her suspicion would have alarmed me; but now I was elevated by my passion above every other consideration. The mistress of my soul having retired with her brother, I discovered so much uneasiness at my situation, that Miss Snapper proposed to go home, and while I conducted her to a chair told me she had too great a regard for me to keep me any longer in torment. I feigned ignorance of her meaning.

The civility of Miss Snapper stands out in sharp contrast against Roderick's incivility, even though the latter is caused by the sudden appearance of Narcissa.

Smollett's use of the "stage passions" conveys the nature of Roderick's immediate emotional state, but it shifts the focus to the context of moral and social relationships. Another ball scene, from *Peregrine Pickle*, further illuminates the effects Smollett's use of the "stage passions" can achieve. Perry, who has been ordered by his beloved Emilia to keep his distance from her, in overcome with jealousy when he thinks she is flirting with another man.

In a word, his endeavours to conceal the situation of his thoughts were so violent, that his constitution could not endure the shock; the sweat ran down his forehead in a stream, the colour vanished from his cheeks, his knees began to totter, and his eyesight to fail; so that he must have fallen at his full length upon the floor, had not he retired very abruptly into another room, where he threw himself upon a couch, and fainted.

As with Roderick, Smollett conveys the nature of Perry's emotional state in formulas that he has applied to various passions: sweat, vanishing color, tottering knees, failing eyesight. Again, however, he is concerned not with the emotional state itself but with its interpretation in terms of a context of significant relationships. In this instance, the traditional comic battle between the sexes forms the context of Perry's jealousy. Perry's collapse follows a pretended flirtation with his dancing partner, a flirtation designed to evoke jealousy in Emilia. His actions, indeed, convince nearly everyone at the ball that he is "in good earnest captivated by the charms of his partner." Emilia, however, recognizes her engagement in the battle between the sexes, for "penetrating into his design," she "turned his own artillery upon himself, by seeming to listen with pleasure to the addresses of his rival, who was no novice in the art of making love." Perry, in contrast, fails to penetrate Emilia's design, so that it is he who fills "his bosom with rage."

Smollett completes his miniature version of the battle between the sexes with a disarmingly oversimplified description of Emilia's fright at Perry's collapse: "Emilia . . . was so much alarmed, that she could not stand, and was fain to have recourse to a smelling-bottle." All possible external marks that could represent Emilia's complex of emotions are here reduced to the single, almost archetypal female act of reaching for smelling salts. Within this context of a comic lover's quarrel, Perry's jealousy is largely redeemed from its inherent pettiness by being viewed as only a particular reflection of a universal comedy, the comedy of social life. In effect, by ignoring the inner workings of Perry's passions, Smollett suggests that the meaning of an individual's internal emotional state derives primarily from its relationship to causes, effects, moral relevancy, and social implications.

Smollett's use of the "stage passions" undoubtedly undervalues the individual's internal emotional state. This undervaluation does not mean that Smollett denies the reality of such a state, but rather that to him, its inner workings are less accessible and, ultimately, less relevant to the total human condition than the individual's life in society. Smollett's "realism" is a realism of characters acting in context. By using "unrealistic" formulas and by applying these formulas indiscriminately to any passion, Smollett sacrifices emotional realism. But as Thomas Wilkes argues, if the actor "confines his studies to Nature in general, and to the passions and manners of mankind in particular, he will be always certain of preserving a close likeness, and never run the hazard of straining himself beyond probability and truth, which may justly be termed Painting beyond the Life." Smollett's characters attempt to be good actors, and while Smollett certainly did not think their internal emotional states were "beyond the Life," he knew that by representing these states through formulas he was at least certain to be painting life. For "the passions are . . . what the keys are in a harpsichord," claims Aaron Hill, and "if they are aptly and skillfully touched, they will vibrate their different notes to the heart and awaken in it the music of humanity." Smollett, through the "stage passions," sought to sound in his characters not the music of the unique individual but the music of humanity.

MICHAEL ROSENBLUM

Smollett and the Old Conventions

Over twenty years ago Nathalie Sarraute designated the times an "age of suspicion": henceforth the serious novelist could no longer rely on the "warts and waistcoats, characters and plots" of the traditional novel since these could only reveal "a reality, the slightest particle of which we are familiar with already." In the same spirit Robbe-Grillet insisted that any art which wishes to continue the "discovery of reality" must purge itself of its dead and dying conventions. But of course for the demanding writer and the demanding reader it has always been an age of suspicion. Although the suspicion of the modern novelist may seem more far-reaching, what he says in defense of his innovations is only an updated version of Virginia Woolf's defense of the Georgian novelist's attempts to go beyond the "warts and waistcoats" of the Edwardians. Or, to move back to the beginnings of prose fiction, a version of the complaints of Encolpius in the *Satyricon* about the numbing effect of the stock tropes of the rhetoricians.

All writers have a stake in the fight against stale convention; certainly the complaints of poets against poetic diction, or dramatists against the formulas of the well-made play are familiar enough. But perhaps the novelist of all writers is the most militant enemy of the old conventions, since the novel (at least according to Ian Watt's influential account) is the genre most committed to a "fresh exploration of reality" without the reliance upon the literary conventions of the past. As Frank Kermode has argued, the history of the novel is a perpetual cycle of novel and anti-novel. The

From *Philological Quarterly* 55, no. 3 (Summer 1976). © 1976 by the University of Iowa.

novelist is always trying to evade "the old laws of the land of romance and the old hero," the conventions of the language of fiction that he inherits. It is not surprising then that the "first" great novel should be a sustained attack on the old hero and the old laws of romance. The writers of the eighteenth century in England likewise found it almost obligatory to begin their works with disparaging references to earlier fiction. Smollett was only being blunter than most when he dismissed romance as an embarrassing survival of the Gothic age: "'Romance, no doubt, owes its origin to ignorance, vanity, and superstition."

But new starts for fiction are not made so easily. The artist may dream of banishing convention and getting directly at unmediated reality, but there is no such thing as unmediated reality in art. As Roman Jakobson pointed out over fifty years ago, the concept of realism is always relative: not only to the norms of the beholder, but also to the existing system of representation which the artist inherits. Thus it is also not surprising that Cervantes should carry out his attack on the old conventions not by *avoiding* them, but by recalling as many of them as possible in his "new" work. It is now a commonplace that romance is not only Cervantes's target, but his great inspiration as well. Similarly, for all their scorn towards the fictional indulgences of an earlier, more childlike age, it was impossible for Smollett or his fellow novelists to banish the old language of fiction from their works. The question is not so much how to avoid romance as how to come to terms with the romance inheritance in particular and the literary past in general.

For the "naive" but still suspicious novelist like Defoe or Richardson there was no problem. Believing that they were imitating reality directly, they allowed their imaginations free play and produced some of the most conventionalized plot formulas of the old fiction: the romance underpinnings of *Pamela* or the incest motifs of *Moll Flanders*. Moreover, they were not bound to the assumptions of the doctrine of separation of styles which decreed that if the story were to be serious, the protagonist must be some version of the old hero, that is, the more elevated hero of epic, tragedy, or romance. For them it was no breach of decorum to give serious and extended treatment to the affairs of servants or middle-class households. On the other hand more self-conscious writers like Fielding and Smollett, more aware of the literary past, could not pretend that their works had nothing in common with earlier traditions. Hence the facetious embarrassment about the protagonist's genealogy in *Joseph Andrews* and *Ferdinand Count Fathom*, the fondness of both novelists for the secret-of-birth social promotion by which it turns out that the hero isn't so "low" after all, and the pervasive mock-heroic stance which protects the narrator in his excursions into low life.

In the preface to *Ferdinand Count Fathom* Smollett defensively anticipates the objections of the reader who may be offended at yet another treatment of "the obscene objects of low life." In the preface to *Roderick Random* he apologizes for his representation of the "mean scenes" in which the hero finds himself. The justification is that the "low state" shows "those parts of life where the humours and passions are undisguised by affectation, ceremony, or education; and the whimsical peculiarities of disposition appear as nature has implanted them." This is very similar to Fielding's claim that "the various callings in lower spheres produce the great variety of humorous characters." For both writers scenes from ordinary life become the material for genre pieces, Empsonian pastorals in which the sophisticated author uses his "primitive" subjects as models for the more complex and therefore more opaque humanity in which he is really interested.

With this outlook neither Fielding nor Smollett is ready to abandon traditional notions of social and literary decorum, even in what they take to be a new kind of writing. Nor will we be surprised if such novelists constantly and deliberately revert to earlier ways of telling a story. Despite his apparent contempt for romance, Smollett rarely gets away from the old hero and the old plots of the land of romance. Even at the most superficial level the debt to romance is obvious: the heroes are from the start presented as extraordinary young men, their specialness being indicated by the early-signs-of-future-greatness formula (the precocity of Random and Fathom), the backward hero formula (Greaves and Melvil), or an alternation between the two, as in the early career of Peregrine Pickle. Only in his last work does Smollett break out of the formula by introducing Humphry Clinker, a backward hero who remains backward. These examples perhaps reveal no more than the persistence of minor narrative fossils. I think, however, that Smollett draws upon earlier ways of telling a story in a more important way: Random, Pickle, Melvil, and Greaves share what could be called a romance mentality, a way of conceiving of themselves and their relation to the outside world that reflects not necessarily their reading of romance (though this is the case with Greaves), but the simple fact that their creator casts his work in the molds of the older language of fiction.

The best place to begin is the opening pages of Smollett's first work of fiction. Random tells how he is restored to the birthright of which he has been cheated, and brought to that state of felicity prophesied in his mother's dreams—that her son would "return to his native land, where he

would flourish in happiness and reputation." All the hero's difficulties begin with the disinheritance of his father by his grandfather for the crime of
marrying beneath his rank. The grandfather is "an unnatural and inflexible
parent," "a merciless tyrant," whose decrees as a judge are "invariable as
the laws of the Medes and Persians." Mother and child are saved by a
faithful old maidservant without whose assistance the mother "and the innocent fruit of her womb would have fallen miserable victims to his rigour
and inhumanity. By the friendship of this poor woman she was carried up
to a garret, and immediately delivered of a man-child, the story of whose
unfortunate birth he now relates." After the death of his mother and the
disappearance of his father, Roderick is left to face his hostile relatives
alone. The more he shows signs of promise, the more Roderick is hated
and envied by his cousins and grandfather. The only help that he gets in
his early years (aside from Bowling's) comes from the poor tenants who
love him because his father was their particular favorite.

Romance archetypes are never far from the surface of Smollett's narrative, but in this account of "the unfortunate birth" they emerge more
clearly than usual. The style throughout is hyperbolic: the grandfather becomes an oriental despot, a Pharaoh, a Herod slaughtering the innocents.
But for Random, who is telling his own story, the language is not excessive. He sees himself as having the birthright and all the gifts of nature
which give him a claim to the hand of Fortune. The typical excess of the
language suggests the extraordinary importance being accorded the
events—as if Random were indeed the hero of romance, or even of sacred
myth. We recognize such classic motifs as the birth in humble circumstances, the help from the lowly in avoiding the wrath of the mighty, the
enmity of jealous siblings as it becomes apparent that the hero has been
chosen to fulfill a special destiny. The immediate situation, boy cheated of
his estate, has been transformed and charged with all the significance of an
anointed prince cheated of throne and patrimony by usurpers. In Smollett
gentlemanhood becomes mythologized, becoming as precious and singular
a condition as being the prince or king in "straight" romance.

Random's experiences in the world are shaped by his gentlemanhood,
the simple circumstance that he is his father's son. When he meets Miss
Williams for the second time he tells her he can choose any "scheme of
life" "without forfeiting the dignity of my character beyond a power of
retrieving it." The essential and permanent part of him, his "dignity of
character," is untouched by experience and cannot be compromised
whether he turn foot soldier or fortune hunter. As Miss Williams tells him,
although his circumstances are low, he is still a gentleman. Since the fact
of birth is irrevocable, gentlemanhood depends neither on present circum-

stances, wealth, or conduct. Because the sense of self is prior to and independent of experience, Random's adventures are separate from what he is, and do not change him into something different than what he has been. Like most of Smollett's other heroes, Random does not really change in the course of the novel. His adventures begin when he is expelled from the paternal estate, and they end when that lost estate is recovered. The time between is therefore a time of exile, a marking of time until the final return to reclaim the estate to which he is entitled.

The framing plot for *Random,* the fictional shape within which all the episodes are "contained," is a very direct adaptation of the typical romance sequence of disinheritance and exile followed by recognition and restoration, and in one way or another this sequence recurs in all the later novels. In *Peregrine Pickle* the hero is in the curious position of trying to reclaim his patrimony from his own parents. The whole situation is wildly implausible since the cause of disinheritance is Mrs. Pickle's unaccountable aversion for her first born and her even more unaccountable preference for her second son. The very great lengths to which Smollett goes in order to bring about the disinheritance suggests his dependence on the romance pattern as a way of giving shape to his narratives. In the third novel, *Ferdinand Count Fathom,* it is Count Melvil who is cheated out of his estate by his wicked stepfather, Count Trebasi. The novel ends with the recovery of the lost estates of Don Diego de Zelos and Melvil. In *Launcelot Greaves* the hero has already come into possession of his estate, and the exile is imposed only by his "madness." In this work, however, it is not necessary for Smollett to insist on the conventions of the romance plot, since Greaves enacts in a literal way the romance assumptions of the heroes of the earlier novels. Only in his last work, *Humphry Clinker,* does Smollett really transform the conventions by parodying them: the social promotion of Clinker is at once unexpected, conventional, and ludicrous since, the revelation of the secret of his birth notwithstanding, Clinker remains a highly unlikely hero. Even though Smollett is being arch about the romance conventions, the point is he still must use them in order to conclude his story.

The protagonist of the romance and the novel may have similar "great expectations," but typically the hero of the novel, unlike his romance counterpart, discovers in the end that his secret dreams of a special destiny are not to be realized. As Ortega puts it, Quixote, the typical hero of the novel, lives in a world in which "the will is real but what is willed is not real." Defoe's Colonel Jacque knows that he is a bastard and is therefore haunted by the possibility that he is of high birth. Although the memory of the romance dream has not been lost (in which all bastards are potentially princes), no romantic Fortune is going to intervene to validate his secret dreams. Whatever social promotion Jacque, Moll, or Pamela get they must earn by their own efforts. For all their talk about the hand of Providence, we can see clearly that it is their own provident natures that make Robinson Crusoe or Moll Flanders so successful. It is only in the special world of romance that what is willed can be converted without effort into the actual. In narratives that we feel to be more "realistic" no supernatural agent, whether it be the hand of Fortune or Providence, can be allowed to tamper with the machinery of causation, suspending the ordinary laws of probability in order to bring about the happy ending. In comedy and tragedy, as in romance, we see a literary kind of fortune, "a wholly extraordinary concatenation of events," a view of life made safer or more perilous under the comic or tragic dispensation.

By contrast, the events and system of causation in more realistic genres such as the picaresque (a genre to which Smollett's works are often assigned) are not extraordinary. However unlucky, the picaro does not see his misfortune as singular since he himself is not important enough to have been singled out for special attention by the gods. Fortune to him is an order of events which results from what Auerbach describes as "the inner processes of the real, historical world." Given the structure of society, the workings of economic cause and effect, the picaro is likely to suffer. But since bad luck is not inexorable, as it would be if it were the expression of the enmity of the gods (as in *The Satyricon* or *The Golden Ass*), it can be sidestepped, and with a little extra effort the picaro can be as successful as a Lazarillo de Tormes. Instead of the image of the relentless wheel of Fortune, we have the mild indifference expressed by Gil Blas when he remembers Epictetus's maxim that Fortune is a whore who dispenses her favors at random.

Although Smollett's heroes may at times have glimpses into the connections between their own fortunes and the structure of society, they more often see themselves as subject to an extraordinary, magical fortune. For them Fortune remains "charged" and personal, the persecution of a cruel Goddess when adverse, and the reward of a kind parent when favorable. When Random finally gets what he wants, he claims that "fortune seems determined to make ample amends for her former cruelty." This imparts a purpose and memory to fortune, as if the probability of a penny landing on heads were to be increased because it had landed on tails for the last forty-nine tosses. Random expects a return of good fortune, a favorable fiftieth toss after the previous consecutive disastrous ones, as no more than his due. The probability of the statistician (who says that the next toss is still just as likely to be tails) is discarded in favor of a universe which keeps track of the tosses. For all the earlier frustrations of the protagonist, the romance fortune in the end implies alignment between will and the world, wish and fulfillment. As in the pathetic fallacy, human feelings are magically projected and reflected in the workings of the external world.

Towards the end of *Roderick Random* and *Peregrine Pickle* both heroes find themselves destitute in prison without any hope of relief. In an education novel this might be the point at which the hero reviews his life and resolves to change. But in both novels there is no introspection and certainly no conversion. On the contrary, the hero does not need to change in order to merit his final reward. Lieutenant Bowling, Roderick's "beneficent kinsman," turns up once more, having in his long absence prospered at sea contrary to all reasonable expectation. He is thus able to convert his beneficence into cash and bail his nephew out. Peregrine Pickle also finds his deliverance from the sea: a ship in which he has invested returns safely. There is no reason why the good luck of Benjamin Chintz the merchant should "reconcile Peregrine to life and predispose him to enjoy human society again," but it does. What reconciles Pickle to life is "this unexpected smile of fortune," the sudden reminder that fortune may be responsive to his wishes after all. One's ship will come in, there are rich uncles, and fortune is neither indifferent nor malign.

Nor is this all. More "magic" is needed to extricate the two young men. Only a completely independent fortune will pass scrutiny and allow Random to marry Narcissa as a gentleman, the only footing on which, by his own vow, he could enjoy her hand. Pickle is equally scrupulous in turning down the offers of assistance made by Pipes, Hatchway, Emilia, and Gauntlet. Only his father's money and estate will serve. Coming into one's own means that the hero is restored to his original condition. He cannot by his own efforts make the restoration come about—he accepts the good fortune as his due. Only with the accession to the paternal estate can the heroes be free, and this can only be accomplished through the most conventional formulas of the world of romance.

The stroke of luck that delivers Peregrine from his perplexity and retrieves his lost estate is the apoplectic stroke that kills his father. Instead of trying to conceal the unlikelihood of his resolutions, Smollett seems to go out of his way to call attention to their artificiality. Nowhere is this clearer than in *Ferdinand Count Fathom,* where the elaborate chivalric stratagems inevitably suggest Tom Sawyer's rescue of Jim. By challenging and defeating Count Trebasi in knightly battle Melville frees his sister and mother and regains his patrimony. The happy ending in *Launcelot Greaves* is equally astonishing: Greaves is fortuitously thrown into the very same madhouse as Aurelia Darnel; Ferret reveals that he is Bridget Marples's secret husband, and thus the entail on Captain Crowe's estate is no longer valid. And finally it is revealed that Dolly Cowslip is the natural child of Jonathan Greaves and thus of sufficiently high birth to be a proper match for Lawyer Clark. As the chapter heading which ushers in all these marvels puts in: "The knot that puzzles human Wisdom, the Hand of Fortune sometimes will untie."

Smollett's favorite means of forcing the hand of fortune is the recognition scene, a staple of literary plots from Homer onwards and one especially favored by writers of romance. Smollett can hardly have been under any illusions as to its novelty, and yet, with the exception of *Peregrine Pickle,* it appears conspicuously in all the novels. Since the first and last (and the most important) of Smollett's novels end with elaborate recognition scenes, it is only a mild exaggeration to say that Smollett's whole achievement in fiction is framed by the recognition scene. And if we can believe the report first given in Moore's *Life,* this was the kind of scene that Smollett liked to stage in his life as well as in his novels. While characters are always reappearing in Smollett, the recognition scene proper is an extraordinary event violating ordinary probability. The most miraculous are those in which two parties related by the closest ties of blood or friendship encounter each other after the greatest possible separation in time and space. The long separation may lead each to assume that the other is dead, and the scene suggests the most dramatic breach of the natural order, the return to life of the dead. The reunion may also bring about a complete reversal of fortune for one or another of the participants. The scene itself is a public spectacle, producing copious tears from participants and spectators alike.

In the recognition scenes between father and son that climax *Roderick Random* and *Humphry Clinker* Smollett turns his back on the demands of realistic fiction and unequivocally writes a kind of fiction in which wish-fulfillment fantasies are not hindered by the reality principle. The reunion between Random and his father in the suitably exotic land of Paraguay has all the improbability of romance; the immediate and mysterious attraction that each feels intimates a hidden relation between them. The revelation that they are father and son is so overwhelming that Random falls into a delirium which brings him to the point of death. He awakens to find his father and uncle hovering over his bed, reborn into a world in which chance is redeemed. The encounter between Clinker and Bramble also conveys the sense that mysterious forces are operating beneath the surface of ordinary events. Because Bramble has saved him from nakedness, hunger, and disease, Clinker promises to "go through fire as well as water" to save

Bramble. And he does go through fire and flood to fulfill his vow—even though the fire at Bullford's is a practical joke and the drowning of Bramble in the ocean is only apparent. But at the very end of the novel Clinker finally gets his chance when the carriage overturns in the stream. As in *Random* there is a "point of ritual death" after which "a *cognitio* takes place, in the course of which their family relationships are regrouped, secrets of birth brought to light, and names changed."

The recognition scene and other cadence formulas make possible the final return of the estate, the event which concludes or is in prospect in all of the novels. What is said of Pickle's journey back to reclaim his estate—it is "the most delightful of all journies he had ever made"—might be said of other return journeys in the novels. At the end of *Random, Greaves,* and *Pickle,* a party composed of the hero and his bride, secondary couples, parents, and parent surrogates stages a triumphal public procession back to the estate, receiving the homage of the local gentry and the adoration of the common people attached to the estate. The solemnity of these processions and the fervor of the tenants suggest the return of an exiled king to his rightful inheritance rather than just the return of a popular landowner.

The estate as final destination in Smollett's narratives has, I think, relatively little to do with the realities of economic life in the second half of the eighteenth century. Smollett's treatment of economic and social forces is for the most part schematic, conveying little of the novelist's interest in the infinite degrees of dependence and independence in society. For his heroes there are only two conditions, vulnerability and security, which correspond to two social classes, the needy vagabond and the independent gentleman. By means of the legal transactions which end *Random, Fathom,* and *Pickle,* the hero has all the signs of his new (old) status conferred upon him. The estate is as mythologized as the condition of gentlemanhood which it defines and the romance conventions which lead to its retrieval. It is viewed through the filters of classical literary myths of Arcadia, Horatian rural retirement, and what may be described as a conservative mythology about orderly societies of the past.

If we think of the eighteenth century as the time of the "rise of the novel," the development of formal realism and the subsequent break with older ways of telling a story, it will be obvious that in returning to the old hero and the old plots Smollett is a writer who prefers to look backward to what is in some ways a discredited language. The lazy or inept writer falls back on the old formulas because he knows they will be acceptable to his "unsuspicious" readers—indeed, they might demand them, and they make his task a bit easier. A romantic closing formula like the recognition scene is in the same category as the wedding and funeral bells which E. M. Forster says providentially come to the aid of the tired novelist. Smollett is not entirely innocent on this score since at times the formulas do seem to be invoked merely to get from one point in the narrative to the next. Often, however, instead of being signs of the perfunctory, the romance language is used to signal the most important transactions in the novel.

The language of romance defines the nature of the journey undertaken in the novels, supplying both starting point and destination. Because of the overall romance shape of the journey, I would suggest that Smollett's affinities with the writers of picaresque have been exaggerated. The picaro can travel indefinitely since there is no natural stopping point: he has no destination, no quest to fulfill which would provide the climax for his adventures. Gil Blas's return to his birthplace is not for him a significant return, and he is soon on the road again, the homeward journey being for him only one of many possible journeys. There is no fixed identity to return to, no patrimony to reclaim. In contrast, Smollett's heroes (and romance heroes in general) are their fathers' sons, and so they do not enjoy, nor would they wish to, the picaro's freedom from the confines of a fixed identity. When they finally return at the end of the novels, they reclaim their proper place in society. For similar reasons it seems to me unsatisfactory to describe Smollett as a writer of education novels. The education novel usually traces the process by which the hero discovers his identity or vocation. In contrast, Random, Pickle, Greaves, and Melville have a conception of themselves which is prior to their experience rather than the product of continuing experience. Smollett's heroes need not discover who they are since they already know who they are and who they will always be. If the hero of the education novel is in the process of becoming, Smollett's heroes are from the beginning already themselves. The end of the novel comes when that identity is confirmed.

I have been suggesting that the romance sequence of disinheritance, exile, and restoration provides Smollett with an "extended fiction," a plot or group of related motifs which serves to unify the total body of an author's work. My next suggestion is one that will be apparent to any reader of Smollett: romance serves mainly as a way of generating a satiric fiction. The romance language brings into focus a world that is the opposite of the idealized and orderly world of romance, the fallen and disorderly world of satire. Smollett updates the old hero and the old plot by insisting upon its anachronism. The heroes are throwbacks to an earlier time, the case of Launcelot Greaves only being a more explicit version of the dislocation of the other heroes. Romance is the language of yesterday which can be made to tell the truth about today only by demonstrating how contemporary reality will not conform to the patterns of romance. The poetic justice required by romance can be secured only by the most outrageous artifice, to demonstrate that gentlemanhood is as anachronistic a condition as the fictional language in which it is expressed. The novelist uses the most contrived of literary devices to make sure that the reader, if not the innocent hero, realizes who it is behind the gifts; only by resorting to an archaic language can one imagine the heroes getting their just deserts. The romance assumptions are exposed to the reader, but not mocked: although romance does not show us how things happen, it does show us the way things ought to happen.

I do not think this sentimentalizes or blunts the force of the satire. Smollett's "realism of assessment" is not compromised by his rejection of "realism of presentation." To the extent that any of the novels makes propositions about the world, they are not saying that a young man of merit is likely to be rescued by a rich uncle, but rather that in the world of the novel which is a model for mid-eighteenth century England, nothing short of a rich uncle can help a worthy young man make his way. For the novels imply another fortune, not the charged, mythological fortune of romance, but the "realistic" fortune that is the product of "the inner processes of the real, historical world," to quote Auerbach once more. It is clear that the fate which these forces contrive is very different from the destiny contrived by the hand of the novelist.

The strategy for Smollett's satire is a very traditional one: romance expectations are played off against what the world is willing to give the hero. Smollett holds the world of desire against the world of experience, the order of gentlemanhood and the inherited estate against the disorder of the society which rejects those values. As Frye reminds us, it is characteristic of satire to contrast the romantic mythical forms with the realistic world which they fit only ironically. Smollett's heroes are a version of one of the classic satiric fictions, the traveller from a purer, simpler world who must voyage through an alien, fallen world. After his time of exile the traveller is allowed to retreat back again into the vanished and timeless world of romance.

Smollett is not a neglected, nor for the most part, a misunderstood writer. He is one of the "Big Five" of the eighteenth-century novel (though almost demonstrably the least of them), and as such he is assured a place on the "required reading lists" of the future—as secure though modest a portion of immortality as a writer of the second rank can hope to obtain.

There is, however, one aspect of Smollett's reputation which could stand some slight modification. A long critical tradition has seen Smollett as a primitive, unliterary writer: a gifted natural the vigor of whose native woodnote wild doesn't quite disguise the fact that he is also singing slightly out of tune. And for most critics the out-of-tuneness is the result of Smollett's deficient sense of form. The rejoinder to this criticism has been very guarded, since Smollett's formal limitations are obvious. It would be tempting to pretend that Smollett was a more suspicious writer than he was, to fashion him in the mold of the very suspicious writers of our own time who seem to know exactly how to mock and exploit literary convention simultaneously. In other words, make him into a writer much like his twentieth-century admirer John Barth, who cunningly ransacks all the myths of the hero and appropriates them for his own purposes in *Giles Goat Boy* and *Chimera*. The claim for Smollett has to be more modest: if he is not as profoundly self-conscious as Barth, rarely is he a sloppy writer falling back uncritically on any available convention. His reworking of romance conventions to construct a satiric fiction suggests that like any other serious writer Smollett had to find a way to use and go beyond the language of fiction that he inherited. Although not as sophisticated as his two contemporaries, the knowing Fielding and the infinitely suspicious Sterne, he nevertheless shares with them a strong sense of the uses to which earlier ways of telling a story might be put.

PAUL-GABRIEL BOUCÉ

The Representation of the Real

Right from the beginning of his literary career, Smollett was aware of the problems posed by the representation of the real in the novel. His preface to *Roderick Random* expresses in very clear terms this prime concern of the author confronted with the choice between a fantastic and fictitious version of life and, at the opposite extreme, a deliberate concentration on everyday existence at its most commonplace, not to say vulgarest. In the first phase, Smollett contemptuously rejects this fallacious vision of humanity and hails with joy the liberating work of Cervantes, whose satirical attacks on it permitted literature to return to the paths of reality and ordinary life. In the second part of this preface, he adopts a tone at once aggressive and defensive. Fortified by the example set by Lesage, Smollett is going to dare to describe scenes which will undoubtedly shock certain readers. The adjectives "mean" and "low" formed part of the critical arsenal of those who were roused to indignation by the liberties taken by Fielding, and even by Richardson, who had the literary courage to be interested in the tribulations of heroes of slender means and humble birth. In his desire to represent reality, the *whole* reality, without omitting the least pleasant aspects of a too often corrupt society, or the physiological necessities of mankind, Smollett declares, in the tone of defiance which is typical of his character: "Every intelligent reader will, at first sight, perceive I have not deviated from nature in the facts, which are all true in the main, although the circumstances are altered and disguised, to avoid personal satire."

From *The Novels of Tobias Smollett.* © 1976 by Librairie Marcel Didier.

Two features are noteworthy in this rough outline, still crude and incomplete, of a literary theory. For Smollett, the representation of the real cannot be dissociated from satire and his moralising purpose. This is why, in the course of this chapter, there will be many references to the satirical vision of the novelist without, however, systematically repeating the observations of the same subject in the previous analyses. Already, Smollett comes up against this problem which, in the nineteenth century, obfuscates all critical discussions on realism. The "realist" writer, in his overwhelming passion for total objectivity, is led to treat subjects which the aristocratic or bourgeois tradition of aesthetic criticism, based on the taste of the ruling class, regards with contempt or even horror. Louis XIV detested the humble domestic subjects treated by Flemish painters. Did he not, according to Voltaire, say "Remove those monstrosities," one day when a Teniers had been hung in one of his apartments?

Smollett's adoption of a literary standpoint in favour of describing far from elevated persons and milieux without repugnance, and his refusal to transform man romantically into pure spirit without imperious and sometimes sordid physical needs, arise, as often in his work, more from a spontaneous and instinctive practice than from a deliberate critical intention elaborated into a rigid theory. In *Peregrine Pickle* he almost contradicts his preliminary statements in *Roderick Random* when he derides this obsession with repulsive pictorial detail of that Dutch painter who has taken great trouble to reproduce an enormous flea on a beggar's shoulder. By taking a satirical line over Pallet's absurd enthusiasm for this picture in which flies are battening on a piece of carrion, he implicitly condemns this meticulous insistence of the artist on a mimicry reduced to the most disgusting detail. In fact, the contradiction is only apparent. Smollett, in this brief passage, has foreseen the dangers of a slavish reproduction of reality, in which the search for an unusual detail takes the place of genuine inspiration. More important on the theoretical plane is the furious reaffirmation, in *Ferdinand Count Fathom,* of his adherence to a concept—free of social or aesthetic contraints and inhibitions—of the novelist faced with contemporary reality. The auto-dedication of *Ferdinand Count Fathom* presents the same mixture as the preface to *Roderick Random*. Its defensive aggressiveness gives a somewhat strident tone to this personal apologia. Smollett replies straightaway in advance to possible (and probable) detractors, that their indignant objections to the "obscene objects of low life" or to the "lowest scenes of life" tend to turn literature into an insipid dish. A certain cantankerous unfairness with regard to illustrious foreign predecessors (from Petronius to Lesage via Rabelais and Cervantes) and English ones (Swift and Pope) gives an unpleasantly polemical tone to this satirical, although courageous, defence of the novelist's aesthetic freedom. Smollett reaffirms his liking for characters of humble origin, in spite of the disapproving snobbery of readers who thoroughly enjoy, in foreign works, what they so strongly condemn in the writings of their English contemporaries. He shows himself fiercely resentful of the criticisms made of his *Peregrine Pickle* and speaks of them with bitterness in his preface to the second edition (1758).

In the *Critical Review,* this concern for authenticity and fidelity to real life which must be reconciled with the aesthetic demands of literary creation also appears on several occasions. In a review of a now totally forgotten novel, the critic—Smollett, according to the conclusions of P. J. Klukoff—insists on the apparent facilities which novelists enjoy for depicting the contemporary world. In fact, these facilities conceal difficulties which are the cause of many failures. After having remarked that the author of *Jeremiah Grant* has not been completely successful in the scenes where the hero experiences the horrors of poverty, he stresses that it requires "the art of a master to exhibit a character in the lowest scenes of indigence, still an object of attention and esteem" (*Critical Review,* January 1763). Supposing that Smollett really did write these lines, could this be an example of a retrospective and personal "puff oblique"? Earlier on, the critic touches on the problem of the representation of the real in its most unsavoury aspects.

> A man may paint a hogstye, or a dunghill very naturally, without giving pleasure to the spectator; and describe with scrupulous exactness many scenes and incidents that produce nothing but yawnings or disgust. It is the happy faculty of genius to strike off glowing images; to seize the ridicule of character, to contrive incidents that shall engage the passions and affections of the reader, to support the spirit of the dialogue and animate the whole. It is the province of taste to regulate the morals of the piece, to conduct the thread of the story, to make choice of airs and attitudes, to avoid impropriety, to reject every thing that is extravagant, unnatural, mean and disagreeable.

Even if the terms "genius" and "taste" are shrouded in irritating vagueness, this passage has at least the merit of clearly stating the selective and creative role of the novelist. This literary transmutation of crude detail into an aesthetically acceptable element had already been emphasised by Lord Kames in his *Elements of Criticism* (1762). At the end of chapter 21, "Narration and Description," Lord Kames asks himself the following question: "An object, however ugly to the sight, is far from being so when

represented by colours or by words. What is the cause of this difference?"
In the case of pictorial representation, Kames explains that the spectator
derives pleasure from the artist's imitation of the reality. As to the literary
description of a hideous object, Kames brings out the importance of language, not only on the plane of social communication but also on the aesthetic plane:

> But nature hath not been satisfied to recommend language by
> its utility merely: independent of utility, it is made susceptible
> of many beauties, which are directly felt without the interven-
> tion of any reflection. And this unfolds the mystery; for the
> pleasure of language is so great, as in a lively description to
> overbalance the disagreeableness of the image raised by it. This
> however is no encouragement to deal in disagreeable subjects;
> for the pleasure is incomparably greater where the subject and
> the description are both of them agreeable.

As Kames's book was very favourably received by the *Critical Review,*
in which several long articles were devoted to it in the March, April and
May numbers of 1762, one is justified in thinking that Kames exercised a
critical influence on the opinions Smollett expressed in the review, already
quoted, of January 1763.

For a quick assessment of Smollett's position in relation to his great
contemporaries, Fielding and Johnson, it is enough to remember that this
problem of reality in the novel was one which frequently preoccupied the
novelist and the moralist. Both insist on the importance, for the author, of
an enriching close contact with the reality of everyday life. In *Tom Jones*
(bk. 9, chap. 1), Fielding recommends the assiduous study of the "vast authentic doomsday-book of nature" as well as the knowledge, not bookish
but human, which an author ought to possess thanks to living in the social
world:

> So necessary is this to the understanding the characters of men,
> that none are more ignorant of them than those learned ped-
> ants, whose lives have been entirely consumed in colleges, and
> among books: for however exquisitely human nature may have
> been described by writers, the true practical system can be
> learnt only in the world.

The caricatural characters of the tutor, Jolter, and the Doctor in *Peregrine Pickle* in some sort confirm the observations of Fielding, who reverts
again to the necessity of a thorough knowledge of *all* ranks of society:

> Now this conversation in our historian must be universal, that
> is, with all ranks and degrees of men: for the knowledge of
> what is called high life will not instruct him in low; nor *é con-
> verso,* will his being acquainted with the inferior part of man-
> kind, teach him the manners of the superior.

Fielding's idea is that society forms a whole, whose various follies are set off against each other. There again, the satirical intention is never far removed, it underlies the representation of the real. Fielding's warning about the insufficient knowledge too many authors have of high society is repeated in chapter 1 of book 14 of *Tom Jones:* "One reason why many English writers have totally failed in describing the manners of upper life, may possibly be, that in reality they know nothing of it." Smollett might (and even should) have profited by this warning, this incitement to caution, from a novelist whose origins and official duties put him in contact with the greatest as well as the humblest. Could it be an echo of Fielding when Johnson, too, in the fourth number of the *Rambler* (March 31, 1750) in-sists, in addition to the importance of erudite knowledge, on "that Experi-ence which can never be attained by solitary Diligence, but must arise from general Converse and accurate Observation of the living World"? He, too, finds that the task of contemporary authors is more difficult than that of the Ancients, for they are "engaged in Portraits of which every one knows the Original, and can therefore detect any Deviation from Exactness of Re-semblance." But this representation of the real is subject to a kind of moral selectivity:

> If the World be promiscuously described, I cannot see of what
> Use it can be to read the Account; or why it may not be safe to
> turn the Eye immediately upon Mankind, as upon a Mirrour
> which shows all that presents itself without Discrimination.

At about the same date, *An Essay on the New Species of Writing Founded by Mr. Fielding* (1751) protests against those who decry the nov-els of Fielding and Smollett as being "cursed low, intolerably vulgar," and, on the contrary, congratulates Fielding on "his thorough Insight into Low-Life." The anonymous author contrasts Fielding's novels with those of his predecessors and never tires of praising the "exact Picture of human Life" and "beautiful Plainness, and exact Similitude" which characterise *Joseph Andrews* and *Tom Jones.*

About the middle of the eighteenth century, there is a confrontation between the partisans and detractors of this fidelity to reality which implies (theoretically) the description of the whole of lived experience. This is a protean problem which, moreover, includes moral (amoral, or immoral) life, flat commonplace everyday life endured rather than controlled, as well as exceptional moments of passionate exaltation or physical decline. Smollett had to endure the assaults of those who were hidebound by a traditional criticism based on the intellectual, aesthetic and social canons of the still dominant aristocracy. Not least of the paradoxes in Smollett's life was that he ranked himself among the conservatives in politics, but among the innovators in literature. So, when his last novel appeared, the *Critical Review* of August 1771 was highly laudatory and rightly appreciated this passionate attention Smollett paid to reality:

> Instead of visionary scenes and persons, the usual subjects of romance, we are frequently presented with many uncommon anedotes, and curious exhibitions of real life, described in such a manner as to afford a pleasure even superior to what arises from the portraits of fancy. We are everywhere entertained with the narration or description of something interesting and extraordinary, calculated at once to amuse the imagination, *and release the understanding from prejudice.*

On the contrary, the *Monthly Review* of the same month saw in *Humphry Clinker* only the risqué and unpleasant aspects (at least reputed such) of this novel:

> Some modern wits appear to have entertained a notion that there is but one kind of *indecency* in writing; and that, provided they exhibit nothing of a lascivious nature, they may freely paint, with their pencils dipt in the most odious materials that can possibly be raked together for the most filthy and disgustful colouring. These nasty geniuses seem to follow their great leader Swift, only in his obscene and dirty walks. The present writer, nevertheless, has humour and wit, as well as grossness and ill-nature.

All through the nineteenth century and even the twentieth, critics have attacked, with the wearisome monotony of inveterate literary spleen, the picture given by Smollett in his novels of a violent world, in which mischievous deeds, gratuitous brutality, debauchery and scatological coarseness appear as so many caustic caricatures of deliberately travestied reality. Smollett, accused of distorting reality by his satirical bias, is rebuked, in the same breath, for the vulgarity, or indecency, of incidents or characters he does not hesitate to include in his novels. The moral aim of his satirical representation of reality is compromised by the literary methods he adopts in the choice and description of subjects banned, at least in theory, by good taste and decency, according to the aesthetic and literary standards of that time.

Any examination of the representation of the real in an eighteenth-century novelist comes up against a problem of literary terminology. How can one speak of the representation of the real without using the word "realism," that paltry critical counter which is almost entirely worthless when applied to the eighteenth century? Used for the first time at the beginning of the nineteenth century in France (1826) and about the middle in England, this term cannot account for the satirical and moral purpose inherent in all representation of the real by Smollett and the other eighteenth-century novelists. A few critics have had the courage to denounce the illicit and noxious use of "realism." C. E. Jones, in his *Smollett Studies* (1942), puts modern readers of *Roderick Random* or other novels on their guard. He emphasises that "realism" is "not only a modern term, but represents a distinction neither considered by the creative artist nor accepted by the critic in the eighteenth century." The same critical prudence is displayed all through the first chapter ("Realism and the Novel Form") of Ian Watt's book, *The Rise of the Novel,* in which the author denounces the almost automatic implication of social and verbal vulgarity which removes a great part of this term's critical utility: "the novel's realism does not reside in the kind of life it presents, but in the way it presents it." As a general rule, "realism" will appear little in this study. After the example of Barbara Hardy in her work *The Appropriate Form,* who substitutes "truthfulness" for "realism," the terms "faithfulness to reality," "authenticity" and even "veracity" will be used. If perchance "realism" (or the adjective "realist") slip into these pages, what must be understood, according to René Wellek's definition, and with the reserves indicated above, is: "the objective representation of contemporary social reality." It is necessary to recall that Smollett's objectivity varies according to the degree of satire, more or less visible and virulent, but hardly ever absent in his representation of reality. For this reason—the indissociability of the satirical and "realistic" elements—it has seemed artificial to conduct two separate studies. On the one hand, many (and indispensable) references have already been made to Smollett's satirical methods in the particular study of each novel. On the other, satire, either in general or in the work of Smollett, has for some years been the subject of a vast number of works. Conversely, there exists no attempt at a synthetic appreciation of the relationship of Smollett's work to the reality of the eighteenth century.

Finally, by "representation," one must beware of understanding a photographic reproduction of reality in its smallest details. This notion, often implicit in the popular concept of "realism," in the end confines the role of the author to the passivity of a sensitive plate on to which the external world is projected. Now all representation of reality can only be partial and incomplete. This is what Joyce Cary expresses, with the vehemence of an author who had himself to endure, *mutatis mutandis,* somewhat the same accusations as Smollett:

> It is not valid to charge a writer with falsification because he emphasises one truth rather than another. As for saying that he does not give the whole, that is absurd because the whole truth cannot be known. It would have to include not only events which are happening all the time and changing the phenomenal world while I speak, but the valuation of events. The most important part of truth is what humanity is suffering, is feeling and thinking at any moment, and this cannot be known, as a totality to any person.

Lukács also emphasises this resigned modesty when confronted with the shifting complexity of the real in his attempt to define the novel as

> a form of mature virility, as opposed to the normal infantility of the epic—that means that the closed character of his world is, on the objective plane, imperfection, and on the subjective plane of the lived, resignation.

The representation is not a simple (!) *transcription* but well and truly a *construction,* indeed creation, according to a critic like Robbe-Grillet:

> Fictional writing does not aim at giving information as does the chronicle, the eye-witness account or the scientific report, but it constitutes reality. It never knows what it is looking for, it has no idea what it has to say. It is invention, invention of the world and of man, constant and perpetually inconclusive invention.

But this modern view, however intellectually attractive, cannot give a satisfactory vision of Smollett's novels in which, very definitely, the part played by social testimony, conscious or unconscious, cannot be neglected. Robbe-Grillet's theory has the merit of suggesting that reality is not an amorphous *datum* preexistent to all literary creation. On the contrary, the novelist, by the creative magic of his word *gives* life to reality. The hellish world of English warships had existed for several centuries, but Smollett was the first who gave it solid dimensions, in a word, the vitality which made it known to the public. Literature and reality are not entities strange to one another and mutually exclusive because of a negative relationship of exteriority. On the contrary, it is necessary to place them on the plane of equivalence, identification or superposition. For Raymond Jean, literature, and the novel in particular, is not mediation but contact, the points of contact between literature and the real being the same as those of our senses with the real:

> There is not the written thing on one side and the real thing on the other: there is a constant dialectical transcendence of this opposition in the act of reading as in the act of writing and this transcendence is a continual creation which enriches life and culture, but also modifies reality and makes it "advance."

These critical prolegomena will make it easier to grasp what must be understood by "representation of the real." If Smollett has left us, consciously or not, a testimony (whose veracity it is the critic's business to assess) regarding the English world about the middle of the eighteenth century, he was also able to create a fictional universe which by very reason of its exaggerations and its satirical distortions seems more real and *is* more real than a flat, didactic type of description. In volume 3 of the *Present State,* Smollett (or an amanuensis) gives a description of Bath and London. But these are dead towns beside those which appear, swarming with life, in *Humphry Clinker.* So, in a first critical survey, the testimony of Smollett on his age will be examined, and in a second complementary one, the limits, characteristics, strengths and weaknesses of the Smollettian universe.

The terms "witness" and "testimony" also leave something to be desired: nothing in Smollett's work or in his letters really warrants the supposition that he was conscious of his role of "witness." But Smollett, whose manifold activities brought him into contact with the most diverse specimens of humanity, even when he was occupied in the historical examination of civilisation and events, nevertheless fulfilled the role of "witness" by the richness of his observations, even fleeting, on everyday life in the eighteenth century. In a way, the first thing with which Smollett provides his modern readers is an involuntary testimony, that is to say a whole series of particulars which retrospectively acquire a historical or sociological value as "facts of civilisation." Often these are hidden details which only a slow, thorough reading, backed by an indispensable knowledge of the civilisation, will cause to emerge from the literary text. Of no particular importance for Smollett's contemporary readers, except as proof of his knowledge of the life of that day, these details constitute for the modern reader, whether English or foreign, a very dense network of historical, sociological, not to mention economic, indications of which it is impossible to analyse more than a few samples.

Thus, when Roderick Random is carried off by the press-gang, he is, according to the heading of chapter 14, on Tower Hill. The specification of place is not without historical interest, for this spot, dangerous for the solitary pedestrian without social protection or official pass, was the oldest and most popular rallying point of the men whose job was to impress men for the fleet. Moreover in that vicinity there were always plenty of disembarked sailors—the favourite prey of the press-gang—who had just collected their back pay from the Navy Office, situated quite nearby. To stay in the nautical realm, Smollett, at the end of *Roderick Random* (chapter 62), makes Morgan, the Welsh ex-surgeon's mate on board the *Thunder,* settle down as an apothecary in Canterbury. This professional transformation is not just a fanciful idea of the novelist's but corresponds to the fact that it was legally possible for naval surgeons, once they were back on land, to obtain an apothecary's licence.

If one leaves the brutal world of the Navy for the more gracious one of women, Smollett draws attention, at least twice in his novels, to the absence, apart from a few rare exceptions, of Latin and Greek in feminine education. In the library of that muddle-headed bluestocking, Narcissa's aunt, Roderick notices that there is not a single Latin or Greek book. Similarly Lismahago, after a long quotation from Ovid, promptly hastens to translate it "in deference to the ladies." Mrs Trunnion's false pregnancy, at once absurd and pathetic, is a gynaecological phenomenon exactly described in popular manuals such as *The Complete Midwife's Practice Enlarged* (fifth edition, 1698). First of all, Mrs Trunnion's breasts harden and her belly swells up, then these apparent signs of pregnancy disappear during three fruitless attempts at parturition so that, after three weeks of false hopes, cunningly maintained by an interested midwife, the unhappy aspirant to motherhood becomes "as lank as a greyhound." The author of the treatise quoted above had already described the same symptoms:

> The face is ordinarily puffed up; the breasts, that at the first were swollen, afterwards become everyday more than other, softer and lanker, and without milk. In fine, the face, the breasts, the arms, the thighs and groyns grow lank and meager; the belly waxes hard, as happens to those who are troubled with the Dropsie.

A few pages further on this same treatise studies the uncontrollable cravings to which pregnant women are subject, and which, allowing for Smollett's satirical intentions, are not unreminiscent of the abnormal cravings of Mrs Pickle.

This involuntary testimony cannot be regarded as an absolutely faithful copy of historical events. Smollett transposes, rather than transcribes. The rebellion led by Peregrine at Winchester does not seem, according to the chroniclers of that respectable public school, to have a factual counterpart, at least at the time when *Peregrine Pickle* was written, though, about 1750, this school was going through a difficult period. On the contrary, Eton had six revolts between 1728 and 1832. So it is not impossible that Smollett attributed the sins of Eton to Winchester, unless the agitation fomented by the real models of Peregrine and his band of mutineers was too usual and commonplace an occurrence at Winchester to merit the name of "rebellion." But it is quite natural for Peregrine to go up to Oxford from Winchester, in view of their historical and administrative links, Wykeham having founded New College in 1379 and Winchester School in 1394. But Smollett does not say whether Peregrine went to New College. The reader of *Humphry Clinker* knows from Jery's very first letter that the latter went to Jesus College, Oxford. There again, the choice is not arbitrary, for this college was founded by a Welshman for Welsh students, as John Macky recalls in the second edition (1722) of his *Journey thro' England:*

> Jesus College for the Welsh, was first founded by Hugh Price, but enlarged by great Benefactions from the *Counties* of Wales since. This college is pretty large, considering the vast number of *Welsh* that come to it, and the President is always a Welshman.

Even if this academic detail ought not to escape a cultured Englishman, it is more doubtful whether the British or foreign "common reader" would grasp the link between Jesus College and Wales at first sight. If the same Macky is to be believed, it is probable that in *Ferdinand Count Fathom* Smollett has reversed the historical connection between the Melvils and Hungary. In his *Journey through Scotland* (1723), Macky observes:

> This family, by the Name, seems to be French; but they say they are *Hungarian,* and came in with Queen *Margaret,* Wife to King *Malcom Kenmore:* However, they are pretty ancient in this Country; for we find Sir *John de Melvil,* of the County of

Fife, one of the Barons that swore Fealty to King *Edward* the
First of *England,* in the Year 1296.

When Macky gives the arms of this noble family he too hesitates over
the spelling and writes "Melvill." Now Smollett states that the old Count
de Melvil, Renaldo's father, "was originally of Scotland." Would this be
a question of a return to his Hungarian genealogical origin for this noble
personage? In any case, it is likely that Smollett remembered the historical
link between the real Melvil family and Hungary when he created his characters of the same name. Another example of adaptation: at the beginning
of *Launcelot Greaves,* Launcelot defends himself against the slanderous in-
sinuations of Ferret who accuses him of being a vagrant. He repeats the
very words of the Vagrant Act of 1744, proving that his affirmation, "I
am not so ignorant of the laws of my country, but that I know the description of those who fall within the legal meaning of this odious term," was
not an idle boast.

Smollett's testimony, even accidental, does not always bear the stamp
of absolute originality; on the contrary it sometimes belongs to a socio-
literary tradition both anterior and posterior to his work. At the beginning
of his stay in London, Roderick is the victim of a "money-dropper," who,
with the complicity of his confederates, fleeces him of all his money. Now
this dirty trick, the character of the swindler, and even his technique, were
no novelty to eighteenth-century readers. Gay (to go back no further) already writes in book 3 of his *Trivia* (1716):

> Who now the Guinea-dropper's bait regards,
> Tricked by the sharpers dice, or juggler's cards?

Is Gay being unduly optimistic or is he taking refuge in rhetorical
irony? A year before *Roderick Random* there appeared a pamphlet, *The
Tricks of the Town Laid Open: or a Companion for Country Gentlemen,*
whose seventeen letters were a scarcely altered repetition of another pamphlet entitled *The Country Gentleman's Vade-Mecum; or his Companion
for the Town,* published in 1699. Letter 13 is summarised thus in the table
of contents: "The Villany of MONEY-DROPPERS is expos'd, and the Ro-
guish Methods they take to impose on Countrymen." In less then four
pages, the anonymous author retraces the history of this swindle which
had been practised for sixty years, its favourite places, and its technique,
which, with a few slight variations, corresponds with the one used to fleece
Roderick. Smollett thus invents nothing new, he is content to adapt a well-
known trick and to insert it, without much difficulty, into the plot of his
novel, Roderick, as an innocent young Scot newly arrived from his distant

homeland, being a readymade victim. But the career of the "money-drop-per" (or "guinea-dropper") does not end with *Roderick Random*. This booby-trap of urban warfare turns up again in the *Extracts from such of the Penal Laws as particularly relate to the Peace and Good Order of the Metropolis* (1768) by John Fielding, the blind magistrate and half-brother of the novelist, who sums it up in a few succinct lines. It reappears in a highly instructive pamphlet dedicated to John Fielding, *Thieving Detected* (1777). The author devoted ten pages to the subtleties of the operation he calls "The Drop" in thieves' slang. The three confederates are called the "Picker-up," the "Kid" and the "Cap," the victim being referred to as "a Flat." No doubt about the same date Richard King wrote *The Frauds of London Detected*, which also gives an exact description of the "money-droppers" and their malpractices. Smollett's testimony therefore links up with a series of writings, of very unequal merit, which enable one to appreciate his fidelity to contemporary social reality. He did not write of this form of swindling from any morbid taste for low life or in order to decry his era, but simply because such fraudulent practices were still common in 1748, and long after.

These few examples of an involuntary testimony which can be drawn from Smollett's work raise the more general problem of the novelist's objectivity. In other words, what part is to be attributed to the observation of real life and what part to satirical distortion? To attempt to solve this problem it was necessary to find a collection of scenes in these novels, sufficiently concrete in detail to provide firm ground for analysis and for which there might also exist irrefutable proofs, warranted by the author's actual participation in the events he describes. It was also necessary to be fairly amply documented on the period in order to compare Smollett's version with that of his contemporaries. Only the chapters in *Roderick Random*, where Smollett, through the medium of Roderick, describes life on board the *Thunder* comply with all these critical imperatives. The purpose of the following pages is not to make yet another systematic study of the British Navy as it appears in *Roderick Random*. It would be futile to repeat the labours of Robinson, Watson, Knapp, Martz, Jones and Kahrl to mention only the most important. The aim of this study is more limited: to analyse the picture Smollett gives of life on board in chapters 24–37 inclusive (over 100 pages) of *Roderick Random*. According to the degree of concordance with contemporary documents it will then be possible to appreciate the discrepancy due to satirical distortion on the triple plane of discipline, living conditions and medical treatment.

Roderick's first contact with naval discipline is characterized by the brutality and gross injustice of Crampley the midshipman who spits on

him, belabours him with blows and has him put in irons. But Crampley
himself soon replaces Roderick in the same decidedly uncomfortable situation, which at least testifies to a rudimentary justice, when the master-at-
arms deigns to exercise it. Smollett emphasises straight away the difference
between the naval officer risen from the ranks, like his uncle Bowling, and
those who owe their rapid promotion to high-placed and influential pa-
trons. The honest tar Jack Rattlin says of Bowling: "None of your Guinea
pigs, nor your fresh-water, wishy washy, fair weather fowls." It is not certain to which of the two categories Captain Oakum belongs. Rumour has
it that he is the brother of a nobleman, but there is nothing to prove that
he owes his rank to favouritism. Although he shows himself an ignorant
and cantankerously vindictive tyrant when Roderick and Morgan are put
on trial, he behaves courageously during the murderous and futile engagement with the French ships. Bowling—and in *Peregrine Pickle*, Trunnion,
another officer who has risen to his rank "by creeping up through the
hawse-hole" as eighteenth-century English sailors used to say—is the
moral and social antithesis of the effeminate Captain Whiffle who replaces
Oakum. Bowling and Trunnion belong sociologically to that generation of
about 1755, described by a naval officer in his *Sailor's Letters*, published
in 1766: "The last war, a chaw of tobacco, a ratan, and a rope of oaths,
were sufficient *qualifications* to constitute a lieutenant" (second edition,
1767). There must also be added, no doubt, for Bowling, Trunnion and
Crowe (although the two latter appear only on land) the technical compe-
tence of these men for whom ships and the sea constituted their sole hori-
zon, sometimes from the age of twelve or thirteen.

That Whiffle, with his sartorial elegance and his homosexual tendencies, represents a type current in the Navy of that time is highly unlikely,
and, after all, difficult to verify. On the other hand, this character belongs
to a dramatic and satirical tradition: the predecessor and perhaps the original of Whiffle, is the sea-dandy Mizen, created by Charles Shadwell in
1710 in the play *The Fair Quaker of Deal*. Edward Thompson altered this
play which was acted at Drury Lane on November 11, 1773. More than
half a century after Shadwell, he only emphasised the fundamental difference between "Commodore Flip," an officer of the old school, a coarse,
heavy-drinking but worthy man, and one of his officers "Beau Mizen."
Flip loathes Mizen with all his might and maintains—but he is the only
one among the group of officers to hold this opinion—that the sailor's profession is incompatible with the status of a gentleman. Dissolute, cowardly
and incompetent, the worst thing about these foppish officers, in Flip's

eyes, is their wanting to live on board in the same luxurious comfort as on shore:

> I hate a fop; it is impossible a fop can be a good sailor, and therefore I hate my lieutenant; the fellow boasts that he does not know the name of one rope in the ship; the puppy too, lies in chicken-skin gloves to make his hands white, and washes them in almond-paste.

Mizen defends himself and it is certain that his arguments met with more sympathy in 1773 than the satirical accumulation of sartorial, cosmetic and olfactory details with which Smollett loads the caricature that Whiffle is. Here is how he replies to his commanding officer's accusations: "Why, commodore, won't you permit a man to be clean! will nothing please you, but what stinks of tar and tobacco!" Finally Worthy, the officer who embodies common sense, condemns the opponents: "Mizen is as great an extreme of absurdity as the commodore." A dated fact will make one realise how slowly the British Navy developed in the direction Mizen desired: soap did not make its official appearance on board warships until 1795. In their excessive refinement, Mizen and Whiffle were the distant literary precursors of an indispensable hygienic measure.

The tyranny of Oakum, absolute master on board, especially at sea when he had to render no account to any higher authority, was not a new feature, either in literature or in the pamphlets of those who had been complaining from the beginning of the eighteenth century of the flagrant abuses of this autocratic discipline. The satirist Edward Ward (1667–1731) does not spare ship's captains, either in his *London Spy* (1698–1709) or, above all, in his virulent and burlesque pamphlet *The Wooden World Dissected* (1707), in which all ranks, from captain to seaman, are ruthlessly lampooned. Ned Ward insists on this tyrannical absolutism of the Captain: "He is a *Leviathan,* or rather a Kind of Sea-God, whom the poor Tars worship as the *Indians* do the Devil, more through Fear than Affection; nay, some will have it, that he is more a Devil than the Devil himself." More caustic still is the accusation of one Barnaby Slush, the probable and appropriate pseudonym of a cook whose indignation impelled him to write *The Navy Royal: or a Sea-Cook turn'd Projector* (1709). Slush attacks pell-mell the incompetent officers, the system of bounties for voluntary enlistment, the unfair sharing-out of prize money, the conditions of life on board, and most of all the intolerable reign of terror established on board by certain authoritarian skippers

who debauch their Power and use it so Tyranically; Tyranically, I call it, since no Slavery is greater than impositions upon
the Mind and Temper of a Gentleman. To be ty'd up to a Ser-
vile compliance with any Fantastick, Hare-brained injunction,
which Pride, or Liquor, shall kindle in the Noddle of a Haughty
Blunderbuss, is worse than shackles.

After Smollett, Fielding, in his *Voyage to Lisbon* (1755), does not display any tenderness for the various officers he meets and the words "tyrant" and "bashaw" recur with indignant regularity to describe their conduct as soon as they feel themselves absolute masters on board. But, unlike
Smollett in the *Travels through France and Italy*, Fielding never fulminates,
and despite his desperate state of health does not collapse into morbid ere-
thism. His portrait of Captain Veal, a petty tyrant terrified, just like Trunnion in *Peregrine Pickle*, at the thought of having a bone to pick with the
lawyers, does not want a certain indulgent sympathy which is lacking in
Smollett.

It is obvious that Smollett has condensed the defects both of the system of recruitment and of the various officers he may have met during his
time in the Navy. Satire cannot have any impact unless the faults it condemns are concentrated in a limited number of characters, who consequently lose most of their specific individuality and become types. So it is
fatal that Smollett's implicit judgment of superior officers such as Oakum
and Whiffle should have been guided by his satirical purpose. The appreciation of his objectivity is rendered all the more difficult because the testi-
monies of his contemporaries on ship's captains by no means agree with
each other. A specialist in British naval history arrives at this balanced conclusion: "Some ships were lax in their discipline, others taut, some officers
were humane and considerate, others were sadists and capricious tyrants."
Thus, apart from the punishment of the cat-o'-nine-tails inflicted by command of the Captain and which was never officially abolished in the British Navy, there were informal corporal punishments on board which could
make life hellish for the members of the crew if a choleric boatswain or
midshipman let themselves go in raining blows with a rattan cane. This is
what happens to Roderick, who gets several stinging slashes from Cram-
ley. This punishment was called "starting" and was the subject of one of
the most usual complaints of ill-treated crews. This practice was only abolished in 1806 but it continued long after. In the case of shipwreck, this
brutal discipline completely broke down. Watson and, after him, Kahrl
have noticed the similarities between the shipwreck of the *Wager* one of

the ships in Anson's expedition, and that of the *Lizard*. Kahrl suggests that Smollett, without being directly inspired by the account given by Bulkeley and Cummins in their *Voyage to the South Seas* (1743) may well have heard the circumstances from the lips of Captain Cheap, the commander of the *Wager*. John Bulkeley, the gunner, and John Cummins, the carpenter, condemn the looters, who, as soon as the ship runs aground, fling themselves on the ship's provisions and the officers' chests:

> we had several in the ship so thoughtless of their Danger, so stupid and insensible of their misery, that upon the principal officers leaving her they fell into the most violent outrage and disorder; They began with broaching the wine in the lazaretto: then to breaking open Cabbins and Chests, arming themselves with swords and pistols, threatning to murder those who should oppose or question them: Being drunk and mad with liquor, they plunder'd Chests and Cabbins for money and other things of value, cloath'd themselves in the richest apparel they could find, and imagined themselves lords paramount.

It is difficult not to compare this passage with the pages in which Smollett describes the same incident on board the *Lizard*. As Smollett remarks, this was a customary proceeding, which John Byron, "Foul-weather Jack," the grandfather of Lord Byron, mentions in his own account of the events which took place on May 14, 1741. This immediate breakdown of discipline in the case of shipwreck is explained not only by obvious psychological causes, but most of all by the following maritime regulation: as soon as a ship is wrecked, the crew's pay is immediately stopped, and, at the same stroke, the authority of the officers and the captain vanishes. In his *Narrative of the Honourable John Byron* published in London in 1768, which furnished Lord Byron with the factual sources for the shipwreck described in *Don Juan*, the author confirms the statements of Bulkeley and Cummins about the behaviour of the crew and lays particular stress on the drunkeness which caused some of them to be drowned in the flooded holds and 'tween-decks. Even before the belated testimony of John Byron, another midshipman in the *Wager*, Alexander Campbell, had published, as early as 1747, a pamphlet less well known than the other two, *The Sequel to Bulkeley and Cummins's Voyage to the South Seas* which also confirms the observations of his predecessors on the behaviour of the crew. Campbell complains of the injustice of Captain Cheap, a choleric man who shot dead another midshipman, Cozens, for insubordination when those who had escaped were trying to survive after running aground on a hostile shore. Cheap, who had arrived in Britain a few weeks before Campbell accused the latter (wrongly) of having defected to the service of the Spaniards, when all he had done was to embark on a Spanish ship. Like the gunner who saved the abandoned *Lizard*, Campbell received neither reward for his loyalty to his Captain nor promotion and even lost his position in the Navy. Confronted with so many concordant accounts, one is forced to conclude that Smollett's description of the scene of the shipwreck of the *Lizard* is in no way exaggerated.

As to the living conditions, right from Roderick's first rude contact with them in the tender which served as a floating headquarters of the press-gang, they are characterized by a persistent impression of vile stench which greets the unlucky Roderick wherever he goes. Tainted provisions, in particular rotten cheese, are the main basic olfactory ingredients of life on board ship. L. M. Knapp's discovery of the diary kept on board the *Chichester* by Lieutenant Robert Watkins states on December 22, 1740, this officer "condemnd Eighteen Hundred and Ninety five pounds of cheese." But this might be just an isolated incident. Such does not seem to be the case, if one is to believe William Thompson's pamphlet *An Appeal to the Public in Vindication of Truth and Matters of Fact* (1761). This former cooper and inspector of the Pickle-Yard, dismissed for the abuses which he indignantly denounced, tried to draw the public's attention to the deplorable quality of the victuals destined for the British war fleet. He reveals in particular

> that seamen in the King's fleet have made *buttons* for their *Jackets* and Trowses, with the *Cheese* they were served with, having preferred it by reason of its *tough* and *durable* quality, to buttons made of *common metal;* and that Carpenters in the Navy-service have made *Trucks* to their Ship's flagstaffs with whole *Cheeses,* which have *stood* the *Weather equally with any timber.*

On the following page he denounces the ship's biscuit, swarming with black-headed maggots, and the beer which stinks like foul water, which does not surprise the reader of *Roderick Random.* As early as 1757 the same author had vigorously denounced, in *The Royal Navy—Men's Advocate,* a sixty-page pamphlet respectfully dedicated to William Beckford, the rottenness of the meat (beef and pork) destined for the sailors, the bad quality of the pickling, the dirtiness of the casks and the corruption of those responsible who ordered the workmen to salt down even stinking carrion. The film director Buñuel could find in William Thompson's pamphlet those horrifying gory details for which he has such a passion, like the piglets escaping from the disembowelled sow in the slaughterhouse, reared by hand and then bled to death in their turn. Another film director, Eisenstein, in *The Battleship Potemkin*, nearly two centuries after *Roderick Random*, managed to recreate this medley of filth and violence with his shots of meat swarming with maggots, his depiction of the men huddled together in the crew's quarters, and the gratuitous brutality of the leading seaman. There is a direct line of continuity from Smollett to Eisenstein, running through Melville, the reformer Melville of *White-Jacket* (1850).

Faecal stenches are added to the odours of putrefaction. It is easy to accuse Smollett of enjoying displaying his olfactory and scatological obsessions, for example in the incident in the sickberth. But once again he is faithful to reality, even in its most malodorous details. This soil-tub, unluckily overturned, is a necessity anticipated in the regulations as early as 1731 and appears in the third section of *Rules for the Cure of Sick or Hurt Seamen on board their Own Ships*:

> The Cooper may, by the Captain's Direction, make out of any old Staves and Hoops, Buckets with Covers, for the necessary Occasions of the sick Men; and if any of them have fractured Bones, or such Ailments as requite their lying in Cradles, the Carpenter may make such a number as shall be necessary.

This mixture of prudent economy and solicitous foresight did not, however, take into account such possible accidents as a sudden heavy roll. It is very difficult to know whether Captain John Blake had ever read *Roderick Random* but, in his very serious *Plan for Regulating the Marine System of Great Britain* (1758), he does not disdain, unlike Smollett's disgusted but futile and narrow-minded detractors, to touch on this problem of general hygiene. Stopping one's nose in the name of a pseudo-aesthetic criticism is no doubt a very refined reaction, but it is not of the slightest practical use. Blake, as a man of experience, knew living conditions on board really well, and proposed the following improvements for the sick:

> That the hospital-room be provided with one or more strong-armed chairs, which may be lashed to the deck, each having in its bottom a close stool-pan made of metal, which may be more easily emptied and washed clean than the wooden buckets directed by the present regulation of the navy to be used, which always retain a smell, though washed ever so clean, and are very inconvenient for a sick man to sit on, frequently overset

with him, by the sudden rolling of the ship, and produce very
offensive and unwholesome consequences; and on such occasions fill the ship with a stench, which not only annoys the
whole company, but retards the cure of the sick, and even contributes to infect those who are well.

Captain John Blake's pamphlet was very well received in the *Critical
Review* of May 1758. In view of such a document which explicitly confirms *all* the details of the scene in the sick bay of the *Thunder,* can one
still talk of satirical exaggeration or excremental obsession? Only the insin-
cerity (or smug ignorance) of a criticism full of contempt for the facts of
civilisation can explain such opinions, though not justify them.

The bad ventilation in these ships with superimposed decks and no air
shafts constituted a problem all the graver because the health of the crew
suffered in these appalling living conditions, especially in tropical zones.
When Roderick realises that he has caught the fever, his first care is to find
a berth where he can benefit from a little air, for the cockpit where the
surgeons lodged was generally situated in the bowels of the ship, often on
the orlop deck well below the waterline. This problem of proper ventilation attracted the attention of the inventor Stephen Hales, who in 1743
published *A Description of Ventilators,* to wit enormous bellows which
would permit the air to be changed in prisons, hospitals and ships of the
fleet and the merchant navy. Like many scientists and doctors of the time,
Hales was convinced that breathing noxious air was one cause of conta-
gion. In his *Treatise on Ventilators* (1758), he summarises the experiments
made on ships in which his cumbrous apparatus had been installed; as
early as 1748, on the *Captain,* of seventy guns, the *Blandford,* a slave-
trader of twenty guns, the *Laura,* and in 1749 on five Nova-Scotian ships.
Another inventor, Samuel Sutton, criticises Hales's bellows in his *Historical Account of a New Method for Extracting the Foul Air out of Ships*
(1757). He had got in touch with the Admiralty as early as 1739:

> In the Year 1739, I was informed that the sailors on board the
> fleet at Spithead were so dangerously ill, for want of fresh air,
> that they were put ashore to recover their health; and the ships
> to which they belonged, stunk to such a degree, that they in-
> fected one another.

Sutton's system was a collection of pipes which went right down to the
hold where a fire was lit to make the air circulate. Sutton received the support of Dr Richard Mead right from the beginning, but, as always, the re-

sistance due to the inertia of ship's captains and officers was hard to overcome. A letter from Rear-Admiral Boscawen to Corbett, dated April 9,
1748, nevertheless shows that, at the very moment when *Roderick Random* came out (January 1748), reforms were already afoot in the British
Navy: "I cannot help thinking, the air-pipes fixed in the men of war have
been of great service in this particular [i.e., of preserving the health of sea-
men], by purifying the air between decks, and thereby preventing the
scurvy."

Even if the conclusion, which conformed with the medical theories of
the day, is erroneous, the effects of this invention, soon followed by other
improvements were beneficial, but obviously it was not installed in Smollett's *Chichester.* So Smollett, far from distorting reality in the interests of
satire, appears as the literary pioneer of a technological reform vital for the
health of thousands of men on board ship.

The representation of the real in Smollett's novels has an undoubted
value as sociohistoric evidence, but cannot be limited only to this function.
Like all human evidence, it shares its brittleness, due to the relativity of
perception. Thus, while Jery and his uncle are indignant about the state of
the roads, a French traveller, Elie de Beaumont writes in 1764:

> The roads of England are beautiful and well-kept. As pedestri-
> ans there are considered to be part of the nation, care has been
> taken to provide a footpath for them, which is usually on the
> right. . . . Signposts indicate the roads with clearly visible direc-
> tions.

But Elie de Beaumont's admiration is explained, in its turn, by the complaints of foreign travellers, and of Smollett in particular in *Travels
through France and Italy,* about the deplorable state of most of the roads
on the continent. The accuracy of details of civilisation is seldom a basic
assumption for the modern reader but has to be reached by a certain
amount of archaeological probing. It is not unimportant that young Wilson disguises himself as a Jewish pedlar in order to try and meet Lydia.
This humble profession was one of the few open to Jews in the eighteenth
century. The vast number of these pedlars—the disguise was therefore a
good one—is explained by racism and the socioeconomic pressure exerted
on his underprivileged, uneducated minority which could not be easily as-
similated by the more civilised Sephardim Jews who had been settled in
London since the middle of the seventeenth century.

Smollett introduces his readers to a world swarming with rogues, crooks, thieves, prostitutes and highwaymen. The critic may be shocked by this display of the more or less sordid sides of the eighteenth century. But Smollett does not show any *complacency* in this description of the underworld, which he surveys in general rather than systematically exploring it. Moreover, he was haunted by the fascinating problem of the interplay of Good and Evil in life and its literary expression. He had already realised that it is impossible to make good literature with good sentiments alone. Conversely, the modern critic who is shocked by Smollett's choice of subjects could (and should) ask himself the following question: in two or three centuries, what idea would these then engaged in research on the twentieth century form after having ransacked the columns of *France-Soir* or the *News of the World* which wallow ambiguously in the depravities of our era? The flat, everyday, commonplace life of Mr So-and-So is a recent literary discovery which Smollett has foreshadowed in *Humphry Clinker* by offering his readers the activities and thoughts of a group of letterwriters who, by their connections and occupations, constitute an analytical cross section of English society about 1765–70.

He runs no risk, however, of becoming bogged down in the boring morass of what, in the nineteenth century, was called the "slice of life," cut from some monstrous, highly indigestible cake. The omnipresent leaven of satire contributes to making his literary pastry more digestible without always avoiding an excess of acidity. The moral preoccupations of satire partly explain why the fresco painted by Smollett in his five novels is not complete, and at least as rich as that of Balzac or Dickens. Smollett suffers not only from the almost inevitable but rather fruitless comparison of his work with Fielding's, but also with the massive work of his openly avowed admirer, Dickens. In fact, it would be fairer to place Smollett among the painters, halfway between Hogarth and Rowlandson. Satire of a personal character (literary and political) belongs henceforth to the abstruse world of erudition. It has lost its brilliance and most of its interest (first and foremost in *The History and Adventures of an Atom*) and shares the same fate as *Le Canard Enchaîné, Punch,* or *Private Eye* a few weeks after their publication; this kind of satire is a dish which needs to be eaten piping hot: the slightest delay renders it flat and tasteless. On the contrary, satire allied to the representation of the real, thanks to the curative virtues of its acidity, presents the occasionally aggressive, but always very lively éclat of a world where social and economic tensions were at once to disappear and revive in the profound upheaval which precedes the Industrial Revolution. Thanks to this mixture, the representation of the real in Smollett's novels has not aged and occasionally even retains a surprising ring of actuality. Two centuries after Matt Bramble, a French writer on gastronomy is denouncing with many specific proofs to support him, the shameful (and dangerous) chemical adulterations to which the capitalist consumer society submits the most everyday articles of food. But, whatever the authenticity and vigour Smollett deploys in his novels to represent reality, this study would be incomplete without the analysis of the structures of the comic which give the Smollettian world its specific literary individuality.

DAMIAN GRANT

Style at the Circumference

Throughout this study I have claimed that in Smollett form is the instrument of style. I must not neglect, therefore, the formal strategy which serves the comic style; the spokes, one might say, that support the rim. Smollett's approach through externals is directed in ways that can be simply illustrated. What typically happens in the comic sequences in his novels is that the details of the situation are registered by the main character— who tends to be the agent rather than the object of the narrative comedy— sense by sense, as if to prohibit the complication of a total response. This elementary comic procedure also enables Smollett to develop the separate strands (or spokes) of each situation, outwards, in a way that heightens the incongruity of the whole.

Early in *Random* Roderick and Strap join up with the waggon making its slow way towards London, and when they try to climb aboard this vehicle meet with the displeasure of Captain Weazel. This scene offers a paradigm of many others that are to follow. Strap it is who approaches first: "but just as he was getting in, a tremendous voice assailed his ears in these words: 'God's fury! There shall no passengers come here.'—The poor shaver was so disconcerted at this exclamation, which both he and I imagined proceeded from the mouth of a giant, that he descended with great velocity, and a countenance as white as paper." However, Roderick musters his courage and climbs aboard, "without being able to discern the faces of my fellow-travellers in the dark": Smollett deliberately restrains

From *Tobias Smollett: A Study in Style.* © 1977 by Damian Grant. Manchester University Press, 1977.

the comedy at the aural—and tactile—level. Strap (who is very much an object of the comedy) is jolted by the carriage, and "pitched directly upon the stomach of the captain, who bellowed out in a most dreadful manner: 'Blood and thunder! where's my sword?' " The captain's wife then joins him in a superior discourse on their situation, which gives Roderick "such a high notion of the captain and his lady, that I durst not venture to join the conversation." However, "another female voice" volunteers a broad mockery of their affectation, and then addresses itself in terms of contemptuous familiarity to a silent companion (" 'Speak, you old *cent. per cent.* fornicator' "), the words "accompanied with a hearty smack" that exacts a "quavering" reply.

After these preliminaries Roderick falls asleep; waking when they arrive at the inn, where he has "an opportunity of viewing the passengers in order as they entered": we move to the visual level. And even here the group is itemised, treated in order. First we have Miss Jenny, "a brisk airy girl, about twenty years old" (the owner of the second "female voice") and her usurer companion, who is more fully described: "His eyes were hollow, bleared and gummy; his face was shrivelled into a thousand wrinkles, his gums were destitute of teeth, his nose sharp and drooping, his chin peeked and prominent, so that when he mumped or spoke, they approached one another like a pair of nutcrackers; he supported himself on an ivory-headed cane, and his whole figure was a just emblem of winter, famine, and avarice." (Smollett refers to this figure as an "emblem" in accordance with the typical comic process of abstraction, to which I shall return later.) It is the captain's appearance, however, that most astonishes Roderick:

> But how was I surprised, when I beheld the formidable captain leading in his wife; in the shape of a little thin creature, about the age of forty, with a long, withered visage, very much resembling that of a baboon, through the upper part of which, two little grey eyes peeped: He wore his own hair in a queue that reached to his rump, which immoderate length, I suppose, was the occasion of a baldness that appeared on the crown of his head, when he deigned to take off his hat, which was very much of the size and cock of Pistol's—Having laid aside his great coat, I could not help admiring the extraordinary make of this man of war: he was about five feet and three inches high, sixteen inches of which went to his face and long scraggy neck; his thighs were about six inches in length, his legs resembling spindles or drumsticks, two feet and an half, and his body, which

put me in mind of extension without substance, engrossed the remainder;—so that on the whole, he appeared like a spider or grasshopper erect,—and was almost a *vox & preterea nihil.*

Here we have one of Smollett's most memorable caricatures, and I shall have more to say about the style of it in a moment. For the present we may at least notice the aptness of the summary at the end: Weazel does indeed "exist" in his voice, he is a sound; and having entertained us with the incongruity of his appearance Smollett reverts to this feature, which is very successfully exploited for the rest of this chapter and the next.

A similar pattern is observable throughout this first novel. When Smollett turns the "visage, voice, and gesture" of the surgeon's mate Morgan to comic effect, Roderick hears him first, and sees him afterwards, in the appropriate order: "we heard a voice on the cockpit ladder, pronounce with great vehemence, in a strange dialect, 'The devil and his dam blow me from the top of Mounchdenny, if I go to him before there is something in my belly—let his nose be as yellow as saffron, or as plue as a pell, look you, or green as a leek, 'tis all one.' " A conversation ensues, very promisingly, for half a page, and only then does Morgan actually appear: "At the same time I saw him come into the birth. He was a short thick man, with a face garnished with pimples, a snub nose turned up at the end, an excessive wide mouth, and little fiery eyes, surrounded with skin puckered up in innumerable wrinkles." But Morgan's physical presence is never as fully realised in the book as his voice.

Smollett uses a similar strategy in the two chapters which relate Roderick's journey to Bath in the stagecoach with Miss Snapper, her mother and a miscellaneous group of other characters, chapters which take us full circle round the circumference of Smollett's style. The reader might also look at the second chapter of *Pickle,* which is literally "invaded" by Trunnion and his associates; and the three chapters in *Fathom* which describe the hero's brief sojourn in prison (39–41), which are another sustained exercise in alternate aural and visual representation, a brilliant transcription in Smollett's most confident and assertive style.

One thing we cannot fail to notice is how often the actual organs of perception are referred to in each case: ears are "invaded" by voices, eyes have "remarkable objects" thrust before them. It is as if Smollett intends to separate the organ in question from any cognitive faculty, using it simply to register an event for comic effect. Ronald Paulson remarks how "in the run-of-the-mill narrative satires of the seventeenth and eighteenth centuries, the Picaresque relationship between two people dwindled to the relationship between an eye and an object," and any of the senses may be similarly isolated to provide the raw material of comedy. Because comedy works through a logical process of abstraction and simplification; the writer uses certain techniques in order to focus our attention on the particular enlarged or elaborated detail he has chosen to emphasise, and thereby to direct our response. the comic imagination operates on life as a prism does on light: it "analyses" experience, reduces it to its constituent parts, which will then appear either grotesque or absurd.

It is clear that Smollett was conscious of this process, from comments that occur in the novels themselves. The effete Captain Whiffle inspects Roderick one sense at a time before he admits him into conversation. "When I entered the room, I was ordered to stand by the door, until Captain Whiffle had reconnoited me at a distance, with a spy glass, who having consulted one sense in this manner, bid me advance gradually, that his nose might have intelligence, before it could be much offended." In a somewhat different context, Smollett describes the condition of being "all ears" when he has the imprisoned hero of *Sir Launcelot Greaves* listen "as if his whole soul was exerted in his sense of hearing" to the voice of Aurelia Darnel in the next cell. And there is a curious passage earlier in this novel where Captain Crowe seems to exploit the stratagem himself to effect a kind of metamorphosis before his hearers:

> As for captain Crowe, who used at such pauses to pour in a broadside of dismembered remarks, linked together like chainshot, he spoke not a syllable for some time; but, lighting a fresh pipe at the candle, began to roll such voluminous clouds of smoke as in an instant filled the whole apartment, and rendered himself invisible to the whole company. Though he thus shrouded himself from their view, he did not long remain concealed from their hearing. They first heard a strange dissonant cackle, which the doctor knew to be a sea-laugh, and this was followed by an eager exclamation of "rare pastime, strike my yards and top masts!—I've a good mind—why shouldn't— many a losing voyage I've—smite my taffrel but I wool—"
>
> By this time, he had relaxed so much in his fumigation, that the tip of his nose and one eye reappeared; and as he had drawn his wig forwards so as to cover his whole forehead, the figure that now saluted their eyes was much more ferocious and terrible than the fire-breathing chimaera of the antients.

Smollett exhibits his technique here very deliberately, as Crowe is first visible and silent, then conceals himself in clouds of smoke in order to speak, and finally reappears—in parts: "the tip of his nose and one eye." His body as well as his language has been dismembered in the process.

If this technique enables Smollett to exhibit his comic creations to best advantage, we need also to consider how these creations are themselves prepared for exhibition. What happens in the prismatic presentation of comic "character" (which word, in this context, seems to require the reservation of inverted commas) is that the stuff of character is thrown out by a kind of centrifugal energy, and reveals itself in "visage, voice, and gesture." "Nature sometimes makes a strange contrast between the interior workmanship and the exterior form," confesses Smollett in the *Atom*, "but here the one reflected a true image of the other"; comedy will normally employ characters who answer to the second description. When Fathom meets Sir Giles Squirrel in Paris he is struck by his manner, which is readily interpreted.

> The baronet's disposition seemed to be cast in the true English mould. He was sour, silent and contemptuous; his very looks indicated a consciousness of superior wealth, and he never opened his mouth, except to make some dry, sarcastic, national reflection: nor was his behaviour free from that air of suspicion which a man puts on, when he believes himself in a crowd of pickpockets whom his caution and vigilance set at defiance: in a word, though his tongue was silent on the subject, his whole demeanour was continually saying, "You are all a pack of poor, lousy rascals, who have a design upon my purse: 'tis true, I could bury your whole generation; but, I won't be bubbled, d'ye see; I am aware of your flattery, and upon my guard against all your knavish pranks; and I come into your company, for my own amusement only."

The meanness of a moneylender who turns up in the same novel is actually conveyed by a sudden distortion of his features: "when the merchant understood the nature of the security, his visage was involved in a most disagreeable gloom, and his eyes distorted into a most hideous obliquity of vision."

The corollary of the idea that character is visible in this way, and may be defined externally, is that it will be expressed in action rather than reflection. As Albrecht Strauss has observed, "Smollett is not the man to linger over subtle Jamesian analyses of states of feeling. Like Fielding and Defoe, he is committed to describing emotional life mainly by its external manifestations." But Smollett's "gesture" is more extreme than that of

Fielding or Defoe. Roderick's resentment is expressed by the knocking out
of teeth, his love by distracted behaviour, and his jealousy by even wilder
demonstrations: "It set all my passions into a new ferment, I swore horrible oaths without meaning or application, I foamed at the mouth, kicked
the chairs about the room, and play'd abundance of mad pranks that
frightened my friend almost out of his senses." Even his conversation is
liable to desert the verbal for the physical level: "To this innuendo I made
no reply but by a kick on the breech, which overturned him in an instant."
On another occasion he is only restrained from kicking the master of cere-
monies at Bath by the fact that his companion (Miss Snapper) gets in first
with a satisfactory verbal rejoinder.

It is in the person of Hugh Strap, Roderick's almost constant companion throughout his travels, that Smollett realises this comic gesture most
consistently. Strap is the very embodiment of the comic style in Smollett;
his every action is characterised by an achieved extravagance and incongruity, from the time he first recognises Roderick while he is shaving the
hero on his way to London—"he discovered great emotion, and not con-
fining his operation to my chin and upper lip, besmeared my whole face
with great agitation"—to the scene at the end where Roderick meets his
father in Jamaica, and his fortune and happiness are assured: "Never was
rapture more ludicrously expressed, than in the behaviour of this worthy
creature, who cried, laughed, whistled, sung and danced, all in a breath."
It is Strap who tumbles into Weazel's guts in the waggon, and gets into his
bed by mistake in the middle of the night; Strap who falls down the steps
into the ordinary, while Roderick is reflecting on the unsavouriness of the
place; Strap who receives the "unsavoury deluge" from a window whilst
Roderick is standing "luckily at some distance" from the discharge. Roderick's misfortunes are often perceived through Strap's reaction to them,
which allows for greater comic possibility. Strap is used to offer an extreme externalisation, as it were, of Roderick's own reactions; fear becomes panic, and distress despair. When they are alarmed at night by the
highwayman Rifle, Strap "crept under the bed, where he lay without sense
or motion"; another highwayman causes him to jump out of the waggon,
and hide behind a hedge. Later he is terrified by a raven, "for his fears had
magnified the creature to the bigness of a horse, and the sound of small
morris bells to the clanking of chains"; he is "quite stupefied with horror"
when he finds out that Roderick has fought a duel, and faints at the sight
of his blood. He lapses into despair with equal precipitation. When Roderick is cheated at cards of all the pair possess he spends that night "involved
in doubts and perplexities"; but when Strap hears the news "the bason in
which he was preparing the lather for my chin, dropped out of his hands,

and he remained for some time immoveable in that ludicrous attitude, with his mouth open, and his eyes thrust forward considerably beyond their station." Roderick perceives Strap's "inward affliction" when "his visage sensibly increased in longitude" after another reverse; and on a later occasion he pauses to remark on his friend's legible countenance: "I never in my life saw sorrow so extravagantly expressed in any countenance as in that of my honest friend, which was, indeed, particularly adapted by nature for such impressions." This specification has been endorsed earlier, when Roderick is recounting to Strap the adventures he has had before meeting with him in France.

> During the recital, my friend was strongly affected, according to the various situations described. He started with surprize, glowed with indignation, gaped with curiosity, smiled with pleasure, trembled with fear, and wept with sorrow, as the vicissitudes of my life inspired these different passions; and when my story was ended, signified his amazement on the whole, by lifting up his eyes and hands, and protesting, that tho' I was a young man, I had suffered more than all the blessed martyrs.

The language of gesture reaches its most extreme here. Strap is "strongly affected, according to the various situations described": his affective centre is atomised rather than analysed by the style, which ensures that the rapidly successive emotions are not resolved into anything. The simple demonstrative verbs ("started . . . glowed . . . gaped . . . smiled . . . trembled . . . wept") have more to do with Smollett's excess of language than with Strap's excess of emotion.

As should be obvious to any reader, there is no question of a relationship between Roderick and Strap, whose persistent devotion to the hero, and unhesitating self-sacrifice in his interest, are a simple reflex of his being. Roderick has told us at the beginning that "The attachment of Strap flowed from a voluntary disinterested inclination, which had manifested itself on many occasions in my behalf, he having once rendered me the same service that I had offered to Gawky, by saving my life at the risk of his own; and often fathered offences I had committed, for which he suffered severely, rather than I should feel the weight of the punishment I deserved." The "relationship" is a mechanical convenience, not a psychological necessity; on these terms, we should not be surprised that Roderick feels in no way bound to his self-appointed servant. Strap is restricted to the cold latitude of comedy, his orbit is out on the circumference, where he is immune through what Bergson calls "insensibilité" to any complication of feeling. Smollett was amused to record that Strap had become "a favourite among the Ladies everywhere"; but he would not have understood Taine's indignation at the treatment meted out to him at the end of the novel.

II

So far I have been concerned more with strategy than style, more with the alignment of comedy than its actual linguistic features; more with the spokes and bearings of the circumference than its actual composition. But I believe there is a necessary connection between the strategy I have been describing—the systematic registering of the external aspect of experience—and the style which carries it out. Only with a remarkable degree of verbal vitality and control can a writer hope to generate the kind of energy which is required to attain the orbit of caricature, and to remain, as it were, weightless in that thin air. Philip Stevick has remarked, very justly, that "locating his energy in his variety of incidents and odd characters tells us nothing about how Smollett differs from, say, Surtees and Captain Marryat, or a considerable number of other novelists who are inventive in that sense but not really worth reading. The difference lies . . . in the remarkably articulated vehicle by which the incidents and characters are conveyed."

The obvious place to start is with Smollett's caricatures, literary creations of startling originality whose like had not appeared in English since the Elizabethan age. Martin Turnell says of characters in fiction generally that each is "a verbal construct which has no existence outside the book"; the truth of this statement is nowhere more obvious than in the case of the caricature, who is conceived at and remains on the level of words, who lives only in a linguistic dimension, never challenging any response on our part beyond an appreciation of his creator's virtuosity. The first notable example we meet in Smollett is Crab, Roderick's original employer.

> This member of the faculty was aged fifty, about five foot high, and ten round the belly; his face was capacious as a full moon, and much of the complexion of a mulberry: his nose, resembling a powder-horn, was swelled to an enormous size, and studded all over with carbuncles; and his little grey eyes reflected the rays in such an oblique manner, that while he looked a person full in the face, one would have imagined he was admiring the buckle of his shoe.

What is immediately obvious is that there is no real attempt to describe here, to make us actually visualise a human figure as a result of reading the words. The caricature is pure verbal gesture, and retains a purely verbal identity. "Five foot high, and ten round the belly" is not a satisfactory measurement but a satisfying phrase, constructed according to a self-contained mathematical logic. The moon, the mulberry and the powder-horn make no attempt to function as actual images, discovering similarity in dissimilars, but become instead obtrusive and outrageous in the degree of dissimilarity they introduce on such a poor pretext of illustration; while the specified angle of Crab's vision is one final fantastic detail that brings the structure to a satisfying climax. Forms like "about," "as if," "it seemed" and "one would have imagined" offer unlimited opportunity for the analogy to fly off into fantasy; these phrases are the typical triggers (in Smollett as well as in Dickens) for some extraordinary invention.

The caricature of Captain Weazel, which I have quoted in another connection earlier in this chapter, is of the same kind. The details do not amount to an actual description, but form part of a distinctly poetic alternative mode, offering an impressionistic verbal correlative to the comic conception in Smollett's mind. The distorted dimensions of this portrait allowed Weazel seventeen inches for his body, once the head and limbs have "engrossed the remainder": which gives to the phrase "extension without substance" a certain plausibility. In his analysis of this description Boucé suggests that the systematic "mensuration" of Weazel gives him "an almost anthropometric aspect"; but it works more as a parody of anthropometry than the real thing. Rather than relating Weazel to average human dimensions, this description expels him from the human centre, casting him in the fixed postures and extreme expressions symptomatic of those characters who are pinned on the circumference.

It would result in needless repetition to deal exhaustively with Smollett's caricatures—quite apart from the fact that they are best encountered in their contexts, where they burst in upon the narrative with all the effect of surprise, rather than in the protective custody of criticism. But in order to place the necessary emphasis on Smollett's verbal imagination, his originality and abundance in the use of words, I shall consider one or two more examples here. The curious assortment of characters Fathom meets in prison (chapters 39–41) are a gallery of caricatures. The Governor himself, Bess Beetle the maid, Captain Minikin, General Macleaver and Sir Mungo Barebones are all animations of the comic cast. Minikin is "equally remarkable for his extraordinary figure and address"; the more developed of Smollett's caricatures, such as Weazel, Morgan, Minikin here, Sir Stentor Stile, Captain Crowe, Lieutenant Lismahago and Hawser Trunnion himself, all have voices to provide, as it were, another plane of existence, though this is still emphatically a verbal one. The figure is made ludicrous through "an extravagant exaggeration of the mode":

> exclusive of the fashion of the cock, which resembled the form of a Roman galley, the brim of his hat, if properly spread, would have projected a shade sufficient to shelter a whole file of musqueteers from the heat of a summer's sun; and the heels of his shoes were so high as to raise his feet three inches at least, from the surface of the earth.

The combination of comic image and absurd extravagance in this description inevitably brings to mind Rabelais, the master of both. The monstrous descriptions in the *Gargantua* are a systematic affront—a comic outrage— to the analogical faculty proper. Consider the extraordinary accretion of ludicrous images that constitute the Anatomy of King Lent: his brain is "of the size, colour, substance, and strength of a male flesh-worm's left ball," "His eardrums like a whirligig . . . the back of his mouth like a porter's hod . . . His ideas like snails crawling down from strawberry plants . . . the base of his spine like a billiard table . . . His breast like a portable or- gan." It is in this tradition of the parodic, detonated image that Ben Jonson compares copulation with the fat trull Ursula in *Bartholomew Fair* to "falling into a whole shire of butter"; that Dickens compares the "ragged, yellow head" of Mr Rugg to "a worn out hearth broom," and his sister's nankeen spots to shirt buttons.

And it is in this tradition that Smollett compares Weazel's legs to "spindles or drum-sticks," and his person to "a spider or grasshopper erect"; Minikin's voice to "the sound of a bassoon, or the aggregate hum of a whole bee-hive"; the wrinkles on Crabshaw's cheeks to "the seams of a regimental coat as it comes from the hands of the contractor"; and even Fathom's constricted situation in the stagecoach (not only caricatures may be treated in this way) to that of "a thin quarto between two voluminous dictionaries on a bookseller's shelf." Such images distract the reader from the subject and compel his attention to the play of the writer's mind itself. They are a kind of intellectual freestyle, a celebration of the voluntary powers of the imagination. Sir Stentor Stile, with his eccentric clothes "ren- dered still more conspicuous by the behaviour of the man who owned them," and a voice "something less melodious than the cry of mackerel or live cod"; the misanthrope Ferret, with his eyes "small and red, and so deep set in the sockets, that each appeared like the unextinguished snuff of a farthing-candle, gleaming through the horn of a dark lanthorn"; the cap- tious Lismahago, his face "at least, half a yard in length, brown and shrivelled, with projecting cheek-bones, little grey eyes on the greenish hue, a large hook-nose, a pointed chin, a mouth from ear to ear, very ill furnished with teeth, and a high, narrow forehead, well furrowed with wrinkles"—all exemplify Smollett's instinct to start his figures spontaneously, out of the resources of language, rather than develop them patiently by observation and analysis. They emerge, as it were, fully fledged from the mind of their creator, and begin to speak and act in a way that is totally predictable.

But no account of Smollett's caricatures would be complete without the support of Timothy Crabshaw, Launcelot's lumpish squire, who is perhaps the most extravagant of them all.

> His stature was below the middle size: he was thick, squat, and brawny, with a small protuberance on one shoulder, and a prominent belly, which, in consequence of the water he had swallowed, now strutted out beyond its usual dimensions. His forehead was remarkably convex, and so very low, that his black bushy hair descended within an inch of his nose: but this did not conceal the wrinkles of his front, which were manifold. His small glimmering eyes resembled those of the Hampshire porker, that turns up the soil with his projecting snout. His cheeks were shrivelled and puckered at the corners, like the seams of a regimental coat as it comes from the hands of the contractor: his nose bore a strong analogy in shape to a tennis-ball, and in colour to a mulberry; for all the water of the river had not been able to quench the natural fire of that feature. His upper jaw was furnished with two long white sharp-pointed teeth or fangs, such as the reader may have observed in the chaps of a wolf, or full-grown mastiff, and an anatomist would describe as a preternatural elongation of the *dentes canini*. His chin was so long, so peaked and incurvated, as to form in profile with his impending forehead the exact resemblance of a moon in the first quarter.

The company at the Black Lion survey Crabshaw "with admiration," but we as readers have the advantage of them; for no such figure could exist as a visual phenomenon. He is wholly a creature of words. Everything in the description is extreme ("remarkably . . . so very . . . manifold") and even the improbable analogies are thrown into extra relief by a special emphasis: his nose bears a "*strong* analogy in shape to a tennis-ball, and in colour to a mulberry," his profile forms "the *exact* resemblance of a moon in the first quarter." The real strength here is in the assertion and confidence of Smollett's style, the exactness in the gauging of that specious precision which accentuates any comic gesture. There is the usual redundancy of epithet ("thick, squat, and brawny"), besides one instance where the adjectives are arranged in a progressive manner: "so long, so peaked and incurvated," the latinate word resounding at the end. And an extra feature here is the comic periphrasis of some descriptive phrases: "a preternatural elongation of the *dentes canini*," that curvature known by the appellation of bandy legs" (this last detail comes later in the description).

These caricatures, then, live at the very circumference of style, where it takes off, relinquishes any responsibility to the real world, and creates its own curve in a condition of weightlessness. Caricature is, in fact, the nearest we can get to "pure style"; the pure style Flaubert dreamed of when he wrote to Louise Colet, using an image which is happily consonant with my own: "What I should like to do is to write a book about nothing, a book with no reference to anything outside itself, which would stand on its own by an inner strength of style, just as the earth holds itself without support in space."

III

I remarked earlier that the more developed of his caricatures have voices as well, and we must pass on to Smollett's dialogue for further illustration of his linguistic facility; of how his imagination functions in the crush of words, and feeds on their fields of energy. The habitual brilliance of his comic dialogue is very original in the novel; neither Defoe nor Richardson ever attempted such a thing, and even Fielding, despite his experience as a dramatist, never created dialogue so idiosyncratic. (Mrs Slipslop is, after all, a very slight example; and Fielding declines the challenge presented by his promising jailbird Blear-eyed Moll in *Amelia* with the lame excuse that her language is "not proper to be repeated here.") Smollett appears again as the honourable antecedent of Dickens in this respect; his marvellous voices adumbrate—and often provide the pattern for—such characters as Jingle, Boythorn and Micawber.

Gary Underwood devotes the larger part of his article "Linguistic Realism in *Roderick Random*" to arguing that Smollett's ability to "recreate peculiarities in the speech of his characters" is an important aspect of his realism, and one in which he is "extremely accurate." But this argument misses, or does not reach, the point: as Underwood himself concedes when, at the end of the article, he quotes Sumner Ives's observation that " 'the author is an artist, not a linguist or a sociologist, and his purpose is literary rather than scientific.' " One is happier, therefore, with Underwood's conclusion that these features (which represent "something new in the English novel") are "not just realistic idosyncrasies; they are often comic. They are another manifestation of Smollett's genius, his ability to fuse the real with the comic and make it one." This genius is amply demonstrated in the extravagant Welsh dialect of Morgan, which provides a rich diversion during Roderick's adventures at sea. Morgan's speech is not acheived by the facile expedient of substituting one consonant for another; Smollett endows him with that kind of verbal luxuriance, and redundancy of epithet, which are the life of a comic character. " 'Got pless my soul!' [Morgan exclaims at his captain's orders], 'does he think, or conceive, or imagine, that I am a horse, or an ass, or a goat, to trudge backwards and forwards, and upwards and downwards, and by sea and by land, at his will and pleasures?' " Morgan is in permanent and voluble dispute with his superiors. He declares to Captain Oakum that he will not be " 'a tennis-ball, nor a shittle-cock, nor a trudge, nor a scullion, to any captain under the sun' " and protests to the effeminate Captain Whiffle that " 'I do affirm, and avouch, and maintain, with my soul, and my pody, and my plood, look you, that I have no smells about me, but such as a christian ought to have, except the effluvia of topacco, which is a cephalic, odoriferous, aromatick herb, and he is a son of a mountain-goat who says otherwise.—As for my being a monster, let that be as it is: I am as Got was pleased to create me, which, peradventure, is more that I shall aver of him who gave me that title; for I will proclaim it before the world, that he is disguised, and transfigured, and transmographied with affectation and whimsies, and that he is more like a papoon than one of the human race.' " On one occasion Smollett introduces an interesting variation by transferring the peculiarities of Morgan's dialect into indirect speech: after another contretemps with the captain he comes down to the berth, "where finding Thomson and me at work preparing medicines, he bid us leave off our lapour and go to play, for the captain, by his sole word and power and command, had driven sickness a pegging to the tevil, and there was no more malady on poard. So saying, he drank off a gill of brandy, sighed grievously three times, poured forth an ejaculation of 'Got pless my heart, liver, and lungs!' and then began to sing a Welch song with great earnestness of visage, voice, and gesture." Visage, voice and gesture: tensors of the taut circumference.

But it is certainly true that Smollett achieves his best effects, in dialogue, with his naval characters—among whom Morgan, like Roderick himself, is only an interloper. From Tom Bowling, who comes to young

Roderick's rescue at the beginning of his first novel, to Sam Balderick, whom Bramble runs into in Bath in his last, these highly original characters offer Smollett a regular series of opportunities to exercise his invention. Bowling's threat to Roderick's cousin (whose hounds he has killed when they attacked him) is promise enough. " 'Lookee, brother, your dogs having boarded me without provocation, what I did was in my own defence. So you had best be civil, and let us shoot a-head, clear of you ... Lookee, you lubberly son of a w——e, if you come athwart me, 'ware your gingerbread work—I'll be foul of your quarter, d——n me.' " And the Lieutenant animates the next three chapters, advising Roderick's grandfather that he is " 'bound for the other world, but I believe damnably ill provided for the voyage,' " scattering the "young fry" that surround this "old shark" with the violence of his denunciation, and consigning them eventually to "the latitude of hell." To the end Smollett managed to invest this idiom with new energy and freshness. Balderick is "metamorphosed into an old man, with a wooden leg and a weatherbeaten face," and his manner of address to Bramble is appropriate to his age. " 'An old friend, sure enough! (cried he, squeezing my hand, and surveying me eagerly thro' his glasses) I know the looming of the vessel, though she has been hard strained since we parted; but I can't heave up the name—' The moment I told him who I was, he exclaimed, 'Ha! Matt, my old fellow cruizer, still afloat!' and, starting up, hugged me in his arms."

But it is Commodore Trunnion himself, after all, who provides the richest examples of Smollett's dialogue, where the exuberance and complexity of the sustained metaphoric language amount to something which many have found it more just to call poetic than comic, ultimately, in effect. There is plenty to choose from, and one must at least mention the celebrated "ride to Church" for Trunnion's wedding (where, as Herbert Read says, "we pass from realism to phantasy") and the commodore's subsequent account of this expedition to the Hunt; but it is at the scene of Trunnion's death, in the middle of the novel, that Smollett let him speak most unforgettably. Peregrine has appeared—a pale figure beside his uncle—in tears; and Trunnion "consoled him in these words":

> "Swab the spray from your bowsprit, my good lad, and coil
> up your spirits. You must not let the top-lifts of your heart give
> way, because you see me ready to go down at these years; many
> a better man has foundered before he has made half my way;
> thof I trust, by the mercy of God, I shall be sure in port in a
> very few glasses, and fast moored in a most blessed riding: for
> my good friend Jolter hath overhauled the journal of my sins;

and by the observation he hath taken of the state of my soul, I hope I shall happily conclude my voyage, and be brought up in the latitude of heaven. Here has been a doctor that wanted to stow me chock-full of physic; but, when a man's hour is come, what signifies his taking his departure with a 'pothecary's shop in his hold? Those fellows come along side of dying men, like the messengers of the admiralty with sailing orders: but, I told him as how I could slip my cable without his direction or assistance, and so he hauled of in dudgeon."

This is much more than "jargon"; Smollett has succeeded in colouring Trunnion's whole expression with a dense network of images, until it seems almost another created language—which can then start using similes again ("like the messengers of the admiralty . . .") as if to form a double layer of analogy. A whole page of counsel to Peregrine follows, and then Smollett reverts to indirect speech for Trunnion's last words, expressing his hope "that, for all the heavy cargo of his sins, he should be able to surmount the foothookshrouds of despair, and get aloft to the cross-trees of God's good favour." Even the pedantic naval commentator who objected to the "extravagant metaphor" of Smollett's naval idiom in general, complaining that it is often "broken by the most violent incongruities," was prepared to applaud this death scene as beyond such literal criticism. Because this is indeed poetry, *poesis*, the making of a new thing in words; and though it may be different from the explosive utterance of Weazel or Stentor Stile it is different perhaps more in degree than kind; a concentration of those techniques, operating on the verbal level, which detain a character in "the pale of Words" in a sense rather different from that Pope intends when he uses the phrase in the *Dunciad*. One of the reasons for the success of such dialogue is that it projects what Bergson called *raideur*, "inflexibility" or comic predictability, in the form of speech. Smollett actually uses this word when he says that Trunnion "was altogether as inflexible with respect to the attitudes of his body" as he was in his patterns of speech, reminding us once again how true was his instinct for the source of laughter.

IV

If caricatures talk, they also move; we can pass on now to consider the effects Smollett attains from the description of comic action. Bergson evades the critical problem here when he says that "verbal comedy should correspond, point for point, to comedy of action and situation; and is only, one might almost say, a projection of these at the verbal level." Because the whole problem is, of course, *how* the verbal level can be made to accommodate the comic gesture; how the comic intention shall translate itself into articulation, and not get diffused in the process. Middleton Murry said that it is a writer's attitude that makes articulate his feeling, for "an emotion which has not the endorsement of an attitude has a trick of dissolving away in the mere act of expression," and this "attitude"— which I understand as a kind of verbal posture, a posture to one's materials continuously implied in the words you use—is absolutely essential in comic writing.

One comes to appreciate, in reading Smollett, that the successful creation of comic scenes requires an extreme verbal fastidiousness and an almost pedantic accuracy. The same verbal energy is required here as elsewhere to keep the circumference taut; the comedy is only effective where a tight circle, not a slack loop, is its geometric image. Consider Smollett's description of Trunnion and his companions on their way to church, as seen by a valet who has been sent out to look for them. "The valet having rode something more than a mile, espied the whole troop disposed in a long field, crossing the road obliquely, and headed by the bridegroom and his friend Hatchway, who finding himself hindered by a hedge from proceeding farther in the same direction, fired a pistol, and stood over to the other side, making an obtuse angle with the line of his former course; and the rest of the squadron followed his example, keeping always in the rear of each other, like a flight of wild geese." The identifying feature of this is its precision, which is largely created by the incongruous use of geometric terms: the troop is "disposed in a long field," crosses the road "obliquely," Hatchway makes "an obtuse angle with the line of his former course." Such language helps to sharpen the comedy, in that the disorder of the scene is paradoxically related in poised and sober prose. The term "stood over" is used in its precise nautical sense (stand over: "to leave one shore and sail towards another"; *OED*), and the concluding simile is both graphic and apt for the occasion.

Just as the success of visual farce depends on exquisite timing, so the successful narration of a farcical episode in words depends upon exquisite verbal tact, poise; the ability to "keep a straight face," verbally, and heighten rather than surrender the comic possibilities. The "Feast in the Manner of the Ancients" in *Pickle* provides an interesting study in the management of a large-scale comic situation. Peregrine is invited to this feast, which is to be presented by the doctor whose portrait Smollett drew from Akenside, along with the doctor's friend (and adversary) Pallet, "a

French marquis, an Italian count and a German baron"—already a promising collection. The point is that the doctor is a pedant (he has been introduced a few pages previously as one "in whose air and countenance appeared all the uncouth gravity and supercilious self-conceit of a physician piping hot from his studies") and intends to model his dinner on the lines of an ancient banquet. At several points in the meal he pauses to describe the ingredients: " 'This here, gentlemen, is a boiled goose, served up in a sauce composed of pepper, lovage, coriander, mint, rue, anchovies and oil; I wish for your sakes, gentlemen, it was one of the geese of Ferrara, so much celebrated among the ancients for the magnitude of their livers, one of which is said to have weighed upwards of two pounds: with this food, exquisite as it was, did the tyrant Heliogabalus regale his hounds.' " This kind of thing recalls another of Bergson's observations, that "humour delights in concrete words, technical terms, precision . . . this is not simply an aspect of humour, but partakes of its very essence." The redundant detail serves as a comic surcharge.

It is the exposure of the doctor's affectation and the exaggerated reactions of his guests that occupies the centre of the stage. When they first approach the table the smell of the various preparations causes the Italian's eyes to water, "the German's visage underwent a violent distortion of features," Peregrine has recourse to breathing only through his mouth, and "the poor painter, running into another room, plugged his nostrils with tobacco." But the best paragraph is probably that which describes in jealous detail how the guests endeavour to dispose themselves on the benches which their host has thoughtfully substituted for "the exact triclinia of the ancients." After "a pantomime of gesticulations" Peregrine and the marquis install themselves:

> The Italian being a thin, limber creature, planted himself next to Pickle, without sustaining any misfortune, but that of his stocking being torn by a ragged nail of the seat as he raised his legs on a level with the rest of his limbs. But the baron, who was neither so wieldy nor supple in his joints as his companions, flounced himself down with such precipitation, that his feet suddenly tilting up, came in furious contact with the head of the marquis, and demolished every curl in a twinkling, while his own skull, at the same instant, descended upon the side of his couch with such violence, that his periwig was struck off, and the whole room filled with pulvilio.

The Italian is deftly dealt with, and his misadventure with the ragged nail, as it were, elided by the syntax: "without sustaining any misfortune, but

. . ."—the intactness of the phrase is juxtaposed in the mind with the torn stocking, and the effect is comic. Also the deliberateness of the delineation ("on a level with the rest of his limbs") contrasts with the absurd uncertainty and tentativeness of the scene described. The baron commits a grosser blunder, which the style interprets almost as a diagram: with the balance of his feet coming up and his head going down; while the final clause, with its satisfying summary "and the whole room was filled with pulvilio," comes rather like the last culminating line of a verse paragraph. The whole scene, we might say, has been picked clean of its comic possibilities by the fine touch of Smollett's prose.

V

Precision, then, one can safely identify as the essential characteristic of comic writing: it "partakes of its very essence." This is the "firmness" that (recalling Donne's compass image) makes the circle just. This it is that generates the articulate energy which is as essential to comic prose as it is to the heroic couplet that Smollett so much admired. And I shall illustrate the special effects achieved through comic precision with a number of passages, sentences or simply phrases taken from the range of Smollett's writing which are marked and made memorable by this quality.

Roderick gives the following account of the culinary arrangements in the medical mess on board the *Thunder*. "The cloath, consisting of a piece of old sail, was instantly laid, covered with three plates, which by the colour, I could with difficulty discern to be metal, and as many spoons of the same composition, two of which were curtailed in the handles, and the other abridged in the lip." The death of the octogenarian captain of the *Lizard* is thus narrated: "he departed in the night, without any ceremony, which indeed was a thing he always despised." Smollett underlines the comic element in an especially vigorous asseveration from Bowling with the ironic phrase that follows it: " 'I trust to no creed but the compass, and do unto every man as I would be done by; so that I defy the pope, the devil, and the pretender; and hope to be saved as well as another.'—This association of persons gave great offence to the friar." After composing his quarrel with Rourk Oregan, Roderick examines the Irishman's pistols and finds that "one of them had been loaded without being primed, and the other primed without a charge." This sentence exhibits the comic mechanism of style at its simplest and most effective: the counterpoint of true absurdity.

When Peregrine quotes from Homer, in conversation with a pedantic doctor, this "self-sufficient physician . . . looked upon his reply as a fair challenge and instantly rehearsed forty or fifty lines of the Iliad in a breath." The prose here (precipitated by the word "instantly") enacts the pedant's automatic reaction as appropriately as it registers the ludicrous hesitation of a philosopher encountered later in the novel, "who seemed to have consulted all the barometers and thermometers that ever were invented, before he would venture to affirm that it was a chill morning," or suggests Fathom's bemusement at the deviousness of a certain lawyer, when he discovers he has "incurred the penalty of three shillings and fourpence for every time he chanced to meet the conscientious attorney, either in the park, the coffee-house or the street, provided they had exchanged the common salutation; and he had great reason to believe the solicitor had often thrown himself in his way, with a view to swell this item of his account." In a particularly energetic phrase, the "ragged attendant" who precedes Major Farrel in his attempt to gain entry to Renaldo's castle is described as "extorting music from a paultry viole."

Greaves provides further examples of this stylistic virtuosity—the achieved completeness and finality of comic statement which, like any art, succeeds by announcing and at the same time fulfilling a purpose. Ferret's character is summarised in its "three peculiarities" as follows: "He was never seen to smile; he was never heard to speak in praise of any person whatsoever; and he was never known to give a direct answer to any question that was asked; but seemed, on all occasions, to be actuated by the most perverse spirit of contradiction." The insistent "never" and the concluding "on all occasions" create a comic impression through their very absoluteness; once again, it is Ferret's *inflexibility* that provides the potential for laughter. At the end of the book Ferret confesses to his imposition as a conjuror in the sharp style which is habitual to him: " 'I did little or nothing but eccho back the intelligence they brought me, except prognosticating that Crabshaw would be hanged; a prediction to which I found myself so irresistibly impelled, that I am persuaded it was the real effect of inspiration.' "

Smollett is less concerned with comic effect in the *Travels,* since most of the absurdities he discovers on the Continent are of the kind that are "too gross to make a thinking man merry," and I shall have enough to say about these [elsewhere]. But the *Atom* reveals Smollett at his most brilliant and inventive, and includes some of his most finished comic fantasy, his most assured comic style. The fantasy works like yeast on what is substantially factual material, and turns the political situation in which Smollett was himself so painfully involved into the "farce of human government"—

the phrase identifies the confident external view—that Smollett invented for his own satisfaction. His determination to retain a consistent ironic distance from materials that had previously engulfed him results in a kind of inversion whereby things about which he does have a passionate feeling are flung to the circumference by the dismissive energy of his style.

We have a vigorous overstatement of the incompetence of the administration under Newcastle: "Here then was the strangest phaenomenon that ever appeared in the political world. A statesman without capacity, or the smallest tincture of human learning; a secretary who could not write; a financier who did not understand the multiplication table; and the treasurer of a vast empire who never could balance accounts with his own butler." We are later invited to believe that under George III "a certain person who could not read was appointed Librarian to his imperial majesty." Enduring Bute's economies, the King's household are "not only punished in their bellies, but likewise curtailed in their clothing, and abridged in their stipends": the two last being the very same verbs, and conveying the same comic attitude, that were used to describe the culinary arrangements aboard the *Thunder* in *Random*. Smollett achieves his decisiveness in part, again, from the astringent use of technical terms. Grenville is described as "an old experienced shrewd politician, who conveyed more sense in one single sentence, than could have been distilled from all the other brains in council, had they been macerated in one alembic"; and a financial enterprise of Pitt's evaporates into smoke "without leaving so much as the scrapings of a crucible for a specific against the itch." But the most conclusive example, where the idea is pinioned and expressed with most exacting, most satisfying completeness, occurs where Smollett is describing Newcastle's fatal inability to say "no": "He never had the courage to refuse even that which he could not possibly grant; and at last his tongue actually forgot how to pronounce the negative particle: but as in the English language two negatives amount to an affirmative, five hundred affirmatives in the mouth of Fika-Kaka did not altogether destroy the efficacy of simple negation. A promise five hundred times repeated, and at every repetition confirmed by an oath, barely amounted to a computable chance of performance." The light of pure intelligence is brilliantly refracted in the precise articulation of this prose, which represents the style of the circumference at its most taut and invulnerable.

One could fill a whole chapter with examples of this style from *Clinker* in the letters of Jery Melford, whose confession of his detached attitude I have used to define my own approach here. Each of his twenty-eight letters is an exercise in comic narration, always amusing, often extravagantly funny; it is Jery's letters, as much as anything else in Smollett, which have created those "peals of unextinguishable laughter" of which Scott wrote. But it is not enough to appeal to the echoes of this laughter: I intend to keep a sharp focus on the prose that occasions it.

Consider the description Jery gives of the guests who come to Smollett's house in Chelsea for his Sunday entertainment. There is one who "had contracted such an antipathy to the country, that he insisted upon sitting with his back towards the window that looked into the garden, and when a dish of cauliflower was set upon the table, he snuffed up volatile salts to keep him from fainting; yet this delicate person was the son of a cottager, born under a hedge, and had many years run wild among asses on a common." Smollett's ridicule of this affectation could not be more comprehensively articulated than it is in these bathetic biographical details. Of another (who suffers from a stutter) the host remarks; "this wag, after having made some abortive attempts in plain speaking, had recourse to this defect, by means of which he frequently extorted the laugh out of the company, without the least expense of genius; and that imperfection, which he had at first counterfeited, was now become so habitual, that he could not lay it aside." The prose is alive with comic implication, and the alertness is due to the use of words ("abortive attempt . . . had recourse to . . . extorted the laugh . . . expense of genius") capable of balancing a fine irony. I shall restrict myself to quoting only one more paragraph: where Jery relates the discomfiture of "a fat-headed justice of the peace, called Frogmore" at the hands of his host's doctor.

> Divers tolerable jokes were cracked upon the justice, who ate a most unconscionable supper, and, among other things, a large plate of broiled mushrooms, which he had no sooner swallowed than the doctor observed, with great gravity, that they were of the kind called *champignons,* which in some constitutions had a poisonous effect.—Mr. Frogmore, startled at this remark, asked, in some confusion, why he had not been so kind as to give him that notice sooner.—He answered, that he took it for granted, by his eating them so heartily, that he was used to the dish; but as he seemed to be under some apprehension, he prescribed a bumper of plague-water, which the justice drank off immediately, and retired to rest, not without marks of terror and disquiet.

The prose here maintains its poise largely through the use of indirect speech, which irons out any untoward exclamation and emphasises the superfluous politeness of a phrase like "been so kind as" in deliberate contrast to the confusion of Frogmore's state of mind. The result is the achievement of a structure which compels us to adopt the attitude of an amused spectator. This is what one calls "comic distance"; the sum of which techniques goes to create the style of the circumference, moving in its untroubled intellectual orbit.

It is interesting to consider the principle which lies behind the typical forms and figures of language used by Smollett in these instances, and indeed throughout his comic writing. This might be described as the determination to construct a curve of statement rather than to betray meaning in the barrenness of a straight line. The tentativeness of "it seems," "probably," and "perhaps": "it seems the hooks that supported this swinging couch were not calculated for the addition of weight which they were now destined to bear"; the withdrawal into the passive voice: the sign of the inn at which *Greaves* opens "was said to exhibit the figure of a black lion"; the deliberate understatement of "*tolerable* jokes," "*some* confusion"—most effectively expressed by the figure of litotes, as when Crab's servant girl informs him that she is pregnant and we are told that "he was far from being over-joyed at this proof of his vigour"; the self-conscious qualification of phrase (in a manner for once reminiscent of Fielding): Mr Pickle's father-in-law, "though he had but little fortune to bestow upon his children, had (to use his own phrase) replenished their veins with some of the best blood in the county"; Lydia Melford's reference to newspapers as "these offices of intelligence, (as my brother calls them) . . ."; the erection of an ironic frame around a word: "that curvature known by the appellation of bandy-legs"; "those animals who lead raw boys about the world, under the denomination of travelling governors"; the use of words of "disproportionate magnitude" and pedantic etymological accuracy: lawyer Clarke, threatened by a bully, "bestowed such a benediction on his jaw, as he could not receive without immediate humiliation"; the kind of "elegant variation" so well demonstrated by Smollett's use (twice) of "curtailed . . . and abridged . . ."; all these are devices employed to avoid the waste of direct statement, and allow that fermentation in the wort of words which makes an idea potent. Think how inert Morgan's three spoons would be if they were simply old, bent and battered: it is precisely the phrase "two were curtailed in the handles, and one abridged in the lip" that promotes them to comic properties.

Again the image of the circumference proves its aptness. There are implications for comedy in Emily Dickinson's lines

Tell all the Truth but tell it slant—
Success in Circuit lies . . .

Directness dissipates, indirectness generates energy: it is like an electrical coil, which increases the charge. Style retains a deliberate distance from the naked, inert and (most intimately) *dumb* idea, creates in the circling labour of speech the very tension by which it lives. Language itself *is* the "beautiful circuiting" Keats described, the intellectual pattern one creates and superimposes on the chaos of total experience.

It is generally true that comic writing will emphasise the form and substance of language itself, the mind's creation, against the experiential flux that seeks to challenge this and break it down. Vocabulary, syntax, rhythm, will all be exploited to achieve the necessary pattern, to cage the world securely in a comic perspective. One is used to the simpler expedients from a selection of writers: Ben Jonson giving us the addict of tobacco who "voided a bushel of soot yesterday, upward and downward," Jane Austen trapping Mr Elton "in the same room at once with the woman he had just married, the woman he had wanted to marry, and the woman whom he had been expected to marry," Dickens recalling, with typical stylistic assertiveness, "the smallest boy I ever conversed with, carrying the largest baby I ever saw," who "offered a supernaturally intelligent explanation" of the former whereabouts of the Marshalsea prison; Henry James relying on the same inherent structures of language to discover Maisie's predicament: "As she was condemned to know more and more, how could it logically stop before she should know Most? It came to her in fact as they sat there on the sands that she was distinctly on the road to know Everything."

Such explicit, obtrusive patterning of experience in language is, we may conclude, intrinsic to comic writing; and we may observe Smollett's systematic exploitation of verbal and syntactic pattern at its most developed in two passages that I have reserved for this purpose. The first occurs early in *Random*, where Roderick relates the injustice he suffered whilst at school.

I was often inhumanly scourged for crimes I did not commit, because having the character of a vagabond in the village, every piece of mischief whose author lay unknown, was charged upon me.—I have been found guilty of robbing orchards I never entered, of killing cats I never hurted, of stealing gingerbread I never touched, and of abusing old women I never saw.—Nay, a stammering carpenter had eloquence enough to persuade my master, that I fired a pistol loaded with small shot, into his window; though my landlady and the whole family bore witness, that I was a-bed fast asleep at the time when this outrage was committed.—I was flogged for having narrowly escaped drowning, by the sinking of a ferry-boat in which I was passenger.—Another time for having recovered of a bruise occasioned by a horse and cart running over me. A third time, for being bit by a baker's dog.—In short, whether I was guilty or unfortunate, the vengeance and sympathy of this arbitrary pedagogue were the same.

Roderick's complaint is delivered with admirable lucidity and rhetorical address; but the examples are so extreme, and so expressed, that our response is one of amusement rather than sympathy. (Smollett knew better than most writers how to animate his reader's indignation; and he also knew that this was not the way to do it.) The charges relating to orchards, cats, gingerbread and old women are made to seem doubly absurd by the way the simple fact of Roderick's innocence is, as it were, embedded in the syntax itself ("never . . . never . . ." etc.), becoming the actual burden of the iteration. The episode involving the "stammering carpenter" is a fantasy of unlikely misfortune, tricked out in all its farcical detail—right down to the specification of the "small shot" supposedly used in the outrage. And the ludicrous idea of receiving punishment for the defensive act of escaping drowning and for the involuntary recovering from a bruise reaches a final pitch of absurdity when punishment is extended to the wholly passive act of "being bit by a baker's dog." The last sentence offers to summarise these misadventures ("In short . . ."), and the way "vengeance and sympathy" become synonymous confirms the fact of Roderick's arbitrary and indeed absurd experience.

My second example comes from *Greaves*. Sir Launcelot, imprisoned in the private asylum, overhears a noisy altercation among the inmates.

This dialogue operated like a train upon many other inhabitants of the place: one swore he was within three vibrations of finding the longitude, when this noise confounded his calculation: a second, in broken English, complained he vas distorped in the moment of de proshection—a third, in the character of his holiness, denounced interdiction, excommunication, and anathemas; and swore by St. Peter's keys, they should howl ten thousand years in purgatory, without the benefit of a single mass. A fourth began to hollow in all the vociferation of a fox-hunter in the chace; and in an instant the whole house was in an uproar—The clamour, however, was of a short duration. The different chambers being opened successively, every individual was effectually silenced by the sound of one cabalistical word, which was no other than *waistcoat:* a charm which at once cowed the king of P——, dispossessed the fanatic, dumb-founded the mathematician, dismayed the alchemist, deposed the pope, and deprived the squire of all utterance.

Here Smollett develops a complicated antithetical movement. The first part of the paragraph is structured very simply, as a numerical list: one, a second, a third, a fourth, allowing for elaboration in the incongruous details (the alchemist with his vibrations, the "pope" with his anathemas); while the last sentence repeats this structure—or rather dismantles it—in an accelerated rhythm, as the different categories of lunatic are successively stripped of their pretensions. The alliterative verbs are particularly well chosen, and satisfyingly progressive in signification. There is a further satisfaction in the amplitude of the final phrase, which again recalls the movement of verse rhythm or the return to the "home" note in music.

It was Coleridge who remarked of one of Smollett's novels that it had "no growth from within." Certainly there is no "within" where Smollett's comedy is concerned, even where the materials it deals with might be available to different treatment. An external view of the world is the necessary condition of the comic style; all lies exposed on the spinning surface, the light circumference, the brilliant rim of the imagination.

VI

I have suggested that comic writing offers a critique of reality. Humour is a province of the intellect, claimed as such by Rabelais when he prefaced the *Gargantua* with the observation

> Mieulx est de ris que de larmes escripre,
> Pour ce que rire est le propre de l'homme

and recognised by Shaftesbury when he asserted that one test of any idea should be its ability to withstand ridicule. Now one of the effects of the simplification of reality by pattern, which I have just been considering, is that it throws into relief the incongruous elements which compose our experience; and by way of conclusion to this chapter I shall look more closely at the techniques Smollett uses to precipitate this sense of incongruity.

In his *Lectures on the English Comic Writers* Hazlitt trained a light on the incongruous which will help us to understand its effect in Smollett's work. "The essence of the laughable," he wrote, "is the incongruous, the disconnecting one idea from another, or the jostling of one feeling against another . . . the ridiculous, which is the highest degree of the laughable, is that which is contrary not only to custom but to sense and reason, or is a voluntary departure from what we have a right to expect from those who are conscious of absurdity and propriety in words, looks, and actions."

Smollett was one so conscious. In a letter he wrote to Dr William Hunter from Nice in 1764 he mentions having seen in a peasant's stable "a starved Ox, a Jack-ass, and a He-goat" and continues, "I mention this assemblage because in passing thro' Burgundy I saw three animals of the same species drawing a Plough very peaceable together." The incongruity of "this assemblage" must have impressed Smollett, since he includes both instances in the *Travels* two years later: "In Burgundy I saw a peasant ploughing the ground with a jack-ass, a lean cow, and a he-goat, yoked together"; In the Cella Sanctior, I found a lean cow, a he-goat, and a jack-ass; the very same conjunction of animals which I had seen drawing a plough in Burgundy." No comment is necessary; it is the nature of the incongruous that it declares itself. All that is needed are the external facts which clash in the mind to produce the desired effect. One feels Smollett must have had these experiences in mind when, a few years later, in the *Atom,* he made use of the following image to expose one of Bute's political stratagems: the idea of "forming an administration equally composed of the two factions, was as absurd as it would be to yoke two stone-horses and two jack-asses in the same carriage."

The perception of incongruity, then, as illustrated here, is one of the mainsprings of the comic intelligence, and one that we find tightly wound throughout Smollett's work. His first novel provides many examples. It is a "voluntary departure from what we have a right to expect" where Jackson confesses to Roderick that "although he had seen a great deal of the world both at land and sea, having cruiz'd three whole months in the channel, yet he should not be satisfied until he had visited France." There is a similar discordance in the details we are given of Roderick's room at the house of the French apothecary Lavement:

> a back room up two pair of stairs, furnished with a pallet for
> me to lie upon, a chair without a back, an earthen chamber-pot
> without a handle, a bottle by way of candlestick, and a triangu-

lar piece of glass instead of a mirrour; the rest of the ornaments having been lately removed to one of the garrets, for the convenience of the servant of an Irish captain, who lodged on the first floor.

It is this free play of the imagination that is put to good use by a sailor from the *Thunder* who affronts the Welshman "by discovering to the people on board that Mr Morgan's wife kept a gin-shop in Rag-Fair" and raising a laugh at his expense. Captain Oregan, from the condition of whose pistols in a duel Smollett has already extracted some amusement, introduces Roderick to two literary compatriots of his whose appearance certainly fulfils Hazlitt's conditions: "But it seems these literati had been very ill rewarded for their ingenious labours; for between them both there was but one shirt and half a pair of breeches." It is the use of the word "literati" here that ensures the effect, from its inappropriateness in such a degraded context. But perhaps the purest examples of incongruity in *Random,* that which most nearly conforms to the surrealists' ideal of pure humour, occurs where Roderick informs us that on a visit to Versailles he "had the honour of seeing his Most Christian Majesty eat a considerable quantity of olives." The dignity of the phrase, and situation, form an extreme, one might almost say a vertiginous contrast with the triviality of the actual information imparted.

Peregrine also exploits the offensive possibilities of incongruity when imprisoned in the Bastille; his trembling tutor finds him "whistling with great unconcern, and working with his pencil at the bare wall, on which he had delineated a ludicrous figure labelled with the name of the nobleman whom he had affronted, and a English mastiff with his leg lifted up, in the attitude of making water in his shoe." The pretensions of the company of philosophers later in the book are similarly routed when Peregrine declares that a medal they have been venerating as an antique is "no other than the ruins of an English farthing." There are several incongruous moments in the prison chapters in *Fathom,* notably the war waged on a table-top between the king of Corsica and Major Macleaver with mussel shells, oyster shells and grey peas, and the fantasy of the "duel by smoking" fought between Macleaver and Captain Minikin. The conclusion of the former encounter at the end of one chapter enables Smollett to begin the next as follows: "This expedition being happily finished, general Macleaver put the whole army, navy, transports and scene of action into a canvas bag"; which sentence represents as comprehensive a dislocation of reality as one can perhaps imagine. *Greaves* is well provided with this dry extreme of humour through the character of Ferret. Ferret's dexterity in defending himself against Tom Clarke's chastisement with a heavy kitchen implement prompts the suggestion that "before he plunged into the sea of politicks, he had occasionally figured in the character of that facetious droll who accompanies your itinerant physicians, under the familiar appellation of Merry-Andrew, or Jack-Pudding, and on a wooden stage entertains the populace with a solo on the salt-box, or a sonnata on the tongs and gridiron." The gratuitous details with which Smollett sketches in this improbable background are meant to suggest the critical destructiveness of Ferret's own intelligence; which is confirmed later in the novel. At one point Ferret appears as a quack doctor offering an Elixir for sale to a crowd of rustics. His rambling, three-page-long harangue is a wild mixture of asseveration and absurdity which recalls Volpone's virtuoso performance as a mountebank in Ben Jonson's play. Ferret disclaims with amazing fertility and irrelevance the successive characters of " 'a felonious dry-salter returned from exile, an hospital stump-turner, a decayed stay-maker, a bankrupt printer, or insolvent debtor, released by act of parliament' " on the way to his climactic affirmation of the virtues of the Elixir itself, which " 'contains the essence of the alkahest, the archaeus, the catholicon, the menstruum, the sun, moon, and to sum up all in one word, is the true, genuine, unadulterated, unchangeable, immaculate and specific *chrusion pepuromenon ek puros.*' "

This climax of absurdity would be enough by itself; but is compounded by the fact that the real motive of Ferret's speech is an attack on the Hanoverian policy of the administration, which keeps breaking through. And indeed the anarchic humour which Ferret provides is oddly related to his political extremism; it is an intrinsic part of his criticism of the political reality of the time. (We may remember that the surrealists employed their own forms of destructive humour very deliberately in order to discredit nineteenth-century positivism and its moral, social, and political superstructure.)

The pursuit of the incongruous is, then, an essential part of Smollett's comic style. One might mention the example (still from *Greaves*) of the confused Dolly setting the kettle on the table, and the tea board on the fire; or the redundant particularity of Farmer Stake's deposition with regard to Crowe, that he saw him breaking the king's peace "with a pole or weapon, value three pence"; or, elsewhere, the superlative accusation made by the Atom to Peacock, that he has been in communication with witches, in particular one "goody Thrusk at Camberwell, who undertook for three shillings and four-pence to convey you on a broomstick to Norway, where the devil was to hold a conventicle."

It is a departure not only from what we expect but from what Lisma-hago himself expects when the girth on his saddle snaps, and his attempt at a gallant salute ends with a tumble in the dust: it is Jery, of course, who is allowed to extract the comic potential from the episode. And one further example at least deserves to be recalled from *Clinker:* the threat of the bookseller Birkin to the unfortunate author Tim Cropdale, that he would serve a writ "if he did not very speedily come and settle accounts with him, respecting the expense of publishing his last Ode to the king of Prussia, of which he had sold but three, and one of them was to Whitefield the methodist"—as if to imply, by this superfluity in the statement of account, that the last transaction was somehow invalid.

After all these examples we can be certain that it was not without mischievous intention that Smollett included the information (in the *Continuation* of his History) that in 1758 the National Debt stood at "eighty-seven millions three hundred sixty-seven thousand two hundred and ten pounds, nineteen shillings and tenpence farthing." The process of computation provides Smollett—as it provided Rabelais and Swift—with a self-inflating, self-detonating image of the alienating effect of the mind's mechanisms in general. The incongruous humour here exposes the suspicious insensitivity of abstract formulation, and symbolic systems, to the implicity judgement of the mind at its most critical, complex and alert: the mind, that is to say, looking in from the circumference.

My discussion of Smollett's comic style has led me into what might at first seem to be inappropriately theoretical areas, towards what Moelwyn Merchant calls "The Metaphysics of Comedy." But the implications of comedy lead us inevitably into such areas; the circumference has its bearing, ultimately, at the centre, and the fact of comedy must be related to our total experience. It is only necessary that we should keep in mind, all the time, the way this or that comic effect actually works, and not become lost in abstract considerations. It is the meticulous attention consistently apparent in his prose that enabled Smollett to attain the position he holds among the few great masters of comic statement in English.

JERRY C. BEASLEY

Richardson, Fielding, and Smollett: Private Experience as Public History

The broad relevance of the various kinds of pseudohistory and historical biography should be obvious to anyone familiar with the works of Richardson, Fielding, and Smollett. Each of these writers styled himself a historian in a fictional mode, and it is easy enough to see that the popularity of their novels coincided with and perhaps was even reinforced by the currency of spy fictions, secret histories, and feigned memoirs and lives of private people whose experience had imparted to them some kind of real public importance. Such works, we will remember, professed to renounce the extravagances of romance, and they contributed importantly to the climate of interest in narrative accounts of familiar life and contemporary affairs, while they almost invariably proclaimed a moral commitment to the ideals of Christian virtue. Throughout their own novels, Richardson, Fielding, and Smollett exhibit their very serious interest in the historical functions of prose fiction. Our labors, said Fielding of his story of *Tom Jones* (in bk. 9, chap. 1)—and his words apply equally well to the two other major novelists of the 1740s—"have sufficient Title to the Name of History," for they draw upon the vast materials furnished to the observant eye by life itself, which is interpreted in these fictions by a transforming moral imagination. The exactness with which the authors of *Pamela, Joseph Andrews,* and *Roderick Random* reflect the texture of life in their period, the social and moral tensions and the actual feel of day-to-day living, suggests the degree to which they shared some of the impulses of the lesser writers, whose works are discussed in earlier pages of this chapter [not reprinted

From *Novels of the 1740s.* © 1982 by the University of Georgia Press.

here]. Their superior gifts and vision enabled them to avoid the limitations of mere topicality and voguishness, but Richardson, Fielding, and Smollett were simply the most able and important among a larger community of writers of prose narrative whose varied approaches to the business of representing the realities of public and private life were mutually reinforcing.

The term *history,* as used in the title of *Tom Jones* or *The History of Clarissa Harlowe,* actually suggested a biographical as well as historical method to readers of the day, and the novels of Fielding, and of Richardson and Smollett as well, possess considerable interest as fictionalized history in both important contemporary senses of the term. Like the popular spy fictions and secret histories, they not only register significant truths about familiar life, but sometimes deliberately enter areas of experience hidden from ordinary view. Fielding and Smollett in particular are satiric writers who aim to expose certain ludicrous or odious people and institutions to their readers' scrutiny and derision.

The heroes and heroines of the major novels are all somehow strangers, at least in a moral sense, to the scenes of wickedness and corruption they encounter. Their resemblance to the moralizing spies of Marana and Montesquieu may well have seemed more than just casual to the first readers of their stories. Always innocent in some degree, characters like Pamela Andrews, Abraham Adams, and Roderick Random are outsiders in the real world, where they are confronted by hypocrisy, venality, and cruelty. The role of Richardson's Pamela, as letter writer and moral agent, is in part that of an observer, a shrewd, articulate, unspoiled country girl whose virtue makes her a kind of alien in genteel society. Here futile efforts to enlist the aid of her captor's neighbors in Lincolnshire reveal the moral shallowness of the country gentry and their upper-class indifference to the rakish carryings-on in their own neighborhoods and their own social circle. In *Clarissa* the picture of life in country houses is narrower than in *Pamela,* but presented in greater depth, and when the novel shifts its scene to London, Richardson bares the inner workings of a circle of libertines and whores as they victimize his beleaguered heroine. The tone of Clarissa's own letters does not differ significantly from that of the epistles written by Mme de Graffigny's Peruvian princess, although they are composed with even greater intensity of personal feeling.

In Fielding's comic "histories" of *Joseph Andrews, Tom Jones,* and *Amelia,* it is the narrator who leads the reader behind the façades of contemporary life, but the effect often approximates that of the spy fictions. In the early scenes of *Joseph Andrews,* for example, the author dramatizes the experience of the innocent and therefore alien hero as a means of exposing the vagaries of Lady Booby and her fashionable household. In the same novel he employs Parson Adams as a device for stripping away the mask of an inept, debased clergyman like the swinish Parson Trulliber (2, 13), and later draws a vivid picture (in 4, 5) of the kind of stupidly depraved country justice with whom Fielding the lawyer was well acquainted and who could, if bribed, "commit two Persons to *Bridewell* for a Twig." Trading justices, in fact, as well as other commonly corrupt public servants (lawyers, physicians, prison bailiffs, clergymen), are from this time abundantly examined in Fielding's fiction.

Smollett's "friendless orphan" Roderick Random, as a young Scotsman, is most definitely an outsider in the scenes that come under his view. Smollett's novel generally follows rather closely the model of Lesage's picaresque romance of *Gil Blas,* but it bears the same relationship to spy fiction as *Gil Blas* does to the same French author's *Le Diable boiteux,* a fantastic adaptation of Montesquieu which Smollett translated in 1750. Roderick lacks the detachment of the typical spy, and his own knavery qualifies his reliability as a witness, but his narrative abounds with graphic accounts of country families in strife, of the follies and vices of provincial pharmacists and innkeepers, the twistings of government bureaucracy, the dishonesty of aristocratic ministers, the machinations of gamblers and fortune-hunters. The extended autobiographical episodes describing the ill-fated expedition to Carthagena in 1741 (chaps. 24–37) supply what is probably the most detailed and damning account ever written of the realities of eighteenth-century Navy life. Smollett's journalistic instincts were strong, and his novel reports with great intensity upon the cruelties of the press-gang, the brutishness of common sailors, the sickening food and the filth of shipboard life, and the incompetence of officers like the *Thunder*'s Captain Oakum and surgeon Mackshane.

The savagely satiric treatment of Captain Oakum, moreover, is a stroke much in the manner of a secret historian as well, for it surely reflects upon some ship's captain, now impossible to identify with any certainty, of the fleet in which Smollett served aboard the *Chichester* during the Carthagena disaster. A number of real people regarded themselves as wounded by the portraits drawn in these episodes, where the author fictionalizes real events for at least the partial purpose of ridiculing public figures. Smollett undertook similar treatment of real-life characters in the long prison chapters of his novel (61–64) where he avenged himself on Lord Chesterfield, who had once denied him patronage, and on Quin, Garrick, Lacy, and Rich, the actors and theatrical managers who had refused to produce his unactable tragedy *The Regicide.* He boldly drew their caricatures in the silly figures named Earl Sheerwit, Bellower, Marmozet, Brayer, and Vandal. It was this "set of scoundrels" who had driven the deserving poet Melopoyn to poverty, despair, and jail.

Like Smollett, Fielding more than just occasionally engaged in a gesture recalling the methods of the secret historian. The Beau Didapper of *Joseph Andrews,* to name but one important example, is clearly John, Lord Hervey, Baron Ickworth, the effeminate, diseased, painted courtier whom Fielding loathed for his loyalty to Walpole, and who was known to his enemies by Pope's contemptuous epithet "Lord Fanny." (Fielding, of course, ironically dedicated *Shamela* to Hervey in the person of "Miss Fanny.") Beau Didapper is that "little Person or rather Thing" who, though immensely rich, chose for the "dirty Consideration of a Place of little consequence" to submit his "Conscience," "Honour," and "Country" to the capricious will of a "Great Man" (4, 9). In this instance, Fielding's intention is identical with that of Mrs. Manley in *Queen Zarah* or the *New Atalantis;* he aims to embarrass a public person and expose him to ridicule, all for partisan purposes.

Fielding probably read the *"Atalantis* Writers" he sneered at in *Joseph Andrews* (3, 1). He certainly despised them, and he would have had no need to turn to them for instruction in the creation of a character like Beau Didapper, or Peter Pounce, or the many other comic figures he drew from real life into the worlds of his fictions for the purpose of ridiculing them. Dryden, Swift, and Pope had all used similar tactics in modes of writing that would have been more likely sources for his inspiration. The point is that the satiric strategies of the secret history were still current in popular fiction, as were the conventions of spy narrative. Richardson, Fielding, and Smollett, as alert members of the reading public, could hardly have been ignorant of these two voguish modes of pesudohistorical writing, or (for that matter) of the degree to which the occasional attractions of their own novels as exposés overlap with the appeal of works like *The Turkish Spy* and *Queen Zarah.* There is no clear evidence to suggest that they borrowed directly from specific conventions of the spy narrative or the *chronique scandaleuse,* but then neither did they, in composing their own works, entirely renounce all association with important attractions of these kinds of popular fiction.

The various forms of historical biography—the lives of all kinds of public figures and of adventurers at sea or on the battlefield—are much more relevant to the novels of Richardson, Fielding, and Smollett than are the spy fictions and secret histories. All three major writers made deliberate attempts to tell stories celebrating the importance of individual men and women, showing how any person, however humble of origin, might rise to a kind of conspicuous moral eminence. Joseph Andrews and Abraham Adams have their counterparts in the Bible, a simple but ingenious allusiveness by which Fielding certifies at once the timeliness and the universal value of their comic experience. The names Tom Jones and Roderick Random in different ways suggest the broad application of the particularized characters they identify and describe—Tom Jones by its very commonness; Roderick Random by its combination of a Christian name drawn from romance and thus hinting at the native nobility of Smollett's hero, with a surname pointing to the dangers of the potentially erratic quality of individual moral life in a vexing, chaotic world. Roderick, like Tom, is projected as a kind of everyman. The epistolary story of Clarissa Harlowe is an intensely autobiographical fiction, and so of course is the first-person tale told by Roderick Random. Yet, as we know from Richardson's emphatic authorial comments, Clarissa herself was conceived as a representative figure whose exemplary function as Christian heroine, in the author's mind, gives her imagined life high public importance. In the novels of all three major writers, whatever their other attributes or uses of popular narrative conventions, private experience as it touches upon the felt reality of familiar life is deliberately rendered as a special kind of contemporary history—moral history, we may call it, or (in the case of Fielding and Smollett) comic history.

None of this is really news. Every modern reader of *Joseph Andrews, Clarissa, Roderick Random,* and the other major novels of the 1740s has acknowledged at least the general appropriateness of their claims to a historical function. Their very first readers were surely just as sensitive to the justice of these claims. But the members of the eighteenth-century audience would have read the novels in a context of popular historical biographies, to which they relate in some very interesting ways, and some of these readers—the more sophisticated ones, anyhow—would therefore have enjoyed an enhanced appreciation of their methods and of their author's performance as contemporary historians in a fictional mode.

There can be no question but that Richardson, Fielding, and Smollett exploited some of the conventions of historical biography, though of course their own complex purposes as artists and as moralists never coincide perfectly with the more limited aims of Simon Berington, or James Annesley, or the author of *Mrs. Christian Davies,* or the other writers of similar narratives. This point may be easily illustrated. The novels of Richardson, Fielding, and Smollett, in pursuit of their didactic purposes, all deliberately employ the motif of the journey, either literal or spiritual as an extended metaphor for life's entanglements. Furthermore, one might argue that each of the major novels subscribes to an idealism that works itself out in the protagonist's moral progress toward a final reward, usually represented by the happiness to be found in a rural utopia. Clarissa Harlowe's reward comes in heaven, of course, but the principle is the same: like Pamela and the heroes of *Tom Jones, Joseph Andrews,* and *Roderick Random,* she ends her journey in a place which, by its very perfections, implies strong criticism of the vexing world through which she has moved. The appeal of this manner of resolution overlaps with the general utopian attractions of a work like Simon Berington's account of the travels of Gaudentio di Lucca, although the kind of ending we find in *Clarissa* had its ultimate origins in pastoral traditions and Christian homiletics, not in utopian voyages, which use a different strategy involving a journey from the real world to a utopia and back again. Clarissa's passage through life to heaven is much more closely related to Christian's journey in *Pilgrim's Progress* than to contemporary travel narratives.

The specifically utopian qualities of the major novels are important, however, and must not be discounted or diminished. Richardson, Fielding, and Smollett were all Christian idealists, though in varying degrees, and surely they were all three aware of the long tradition and continued currency of utopian travel literature, which may have at least indirectly influenced their vision of the meaning of their characters' experience. A more cautious comment, perhaps, is that their Christian understanding of moral life coincided with the idealism expressed in utopian narrative, and that this very real parallel may have been to some degree deliberately emphasized in their novels as an ingredient of their formula for popular success. We may only speculate whether this is so, but the very obviousness of the parallel must have helped to fire the enthusiasm of contemporary readers long since accustomed to the pleasures of utopian tales and to other kinds of stories—the pious novels of Penelope Aubin, for example—that resolved the crises of their beleaguered heroes and heroines' progress toward fulfillment by imposing a Christian utopian vision upon the hard empirical realities of their fictional worlds.

Other kinds of adventure narratives bear much more directly on the practice of the major novelists. In *Jonathan Wild,* Mrs. Heartfree's long story of her scarifying experiences with her abductor Wild, of her escape and subsequent adventures on high seas and foreign shores, is Fielding's tongue-in-cheek version of a conventional imaginary voyage. Wild's own adventures after Mrs. Heartfree's departure burlesque the same mode. Earlier in the book Fielding parodies the Grand Tour (and its literature) by devoting to his "hero's" travels the less than two pages of a "very short chapter" containing "not one adventure worthy the reader's notice." In his

Journal of a Voyage to Lisbon (1755), Fielding would offer a voyage narrative worthy of admiration, as he declared in the preface, because not disfigured either by the introduction of monsters and improbable adventures in unimaginable places, or by the dilation of trivial experience into many dull pages. The voyage narrative, Fielding explained, as a species of historical writing, ought to tell the truth, it ought to be artfully done, and it ought to instruct as well as delight. In *Jonathan Wild* he sought, as did Swift in *Gulliver's Travels,* to expose some of the absurdities of familiar voyage and travel literature. And yet Fielding's purpose, like Swift's, was more complex. By the extravagance and vanities of Mrs. Heartfree's tale, he obviously meant to mix in some foibles that would qualify her otherwise unblemished character, thus bringing it closer to his own theories of characterization. At the same time, he was perfectly serious at another level. Mrs. Heartfree's tale of her trials—of abduction, slavery, leering advances, attempted rape, and so on—illustrates her moral strength and functions as a parable of persecuted virtue triumphant.

Fielding's two great novels of the 1740s, the histories of Joseph Andrews and Tom Jones, present stories of energetic adventurers possessing great personal resilience and powerful moral and emotional interest as ordinary people struggling through life's entanglements. Because the aims of these two works are so very complex, they far surpass anything achieved by the author of the historical biography of Mother Ross or by James Annesley in his autobiographical *Memoirs of an Unfortunate Young Nobleman.* But *Joseph Andrews* and *Tom Jones* do deliberately incorporate some of the same interests as these lesser works. *Tom Jones* does so most conspicuously. The novel is sprinkled with allusions to the Jacobites, and Tom's escapades on the road to London are actually thrown into relief against the turbulent background of the 'Forty-Five. Fielding's lively youth even joins the Hanoverian cause as a soldier ready to die in order to protect the kingdom from the Jacobite invaders. This is all obvious. But the important thing is that for a time at least, the very identity of Tom as familiar hero is partly defined by his direct connection with a great public controversy.

In his last novel, *Amelia,* Fielding exploits still more conspicuously the appeal of the popular historical biographies of military characters in treating the experience of his wayward soldier Billy Booth. Booth is the central figure in a considerable cast of military characters. Though weak and vacillating in his domestic relations, he is a responsible officer who fights valiantly and is wounded at Gibraltar. We see only slightly more of Booth's actual soldiering than we do of Tom Jones's experiences as a military man,

but we are led to believe that he was courageous. It is of course impossible
to know the degree to which Fielding may have intentionally tried to call
to mind the many fashionable tales of soldiering adventurers, but to any
reasonably alert reader *Amelia* must have seemed more than just remotely
related to works like *Mrs. Davies* and Defoe's *Memoirs of a Cavalier*. Fielding's novel effectually turns the formula of the military memoir inside
out. The hero's adventures occur mainly in Admiralty offices and the prisons and coffee houses of London, and his enemies are mostly domestic.
But the specific effect of the novel's treatment of this gallant soldier is toward defining a higher kind of heroism. Booth, an ordinary man who has
benefited from hard experience and finally from the wisdom of Isaac Bar-
row's sermons, achieves in the teeming world of London what he could
not attain in the isolated, remote world of the battlefield, where the dangers were only physical: the status of a Christian hero. In fact, Fielding
seems to say in *Amelia* that the real battles, the important moral struggles,
are fought in the everyday world, and it is there that they must be won.
The circumstances of Booth's seemingly hopeless poverty and his terrible
frustrations in trying to get a promotion expose the abuses of privilege in
the prevailing military system, and therefore function in the fabric of the
novel's social criticism. They link the world of the battlefield with that of
daily affairs, which is the novel's main arena, and thus join with Fielding's
exposure of a large variety of other social ills—corrupt justices, prison
abuses, official favoritism, inadequacies and cruel inequities in the treatment of debtors, the irresponsibilities of an indifferent aristocracy, and so
on—in defining the world's resistance to goodness and charity. By surviving his adventures, Booth actually becomes not a warrior hero but, in a
very rich sense indeed, a Christian soldier and thus a triumphant figure important to our understanding of Fielding's conception of the deepest meaning of heroism and of his own role as moral historian in a vein of comic
fiction.

In *Roderick Random* and *Peregrine Pickle,* with their large casts of
fighting sailors, Smollett approaches more nearly than Fielding ever does
the actual formula of popular military memoirs. Smollett is a kind of pan-
oramist, and his sailors are less subtly drawn than the soldiers in *Amelia*.
Not one of them possesses the depth of Billy Booth, although Peregrine
Pickle's benefactor Commodore Hawser Trunnion, in all his delightfully
grotesque eccentricities, belongs among the most memorable military characters in eighteenth-century fiction. But Smollett's sailors were drawn from
firsthand observation, and what they lack in subtlety is made up for by the
accuracy and vividness of the portraits. The shipboard scenes of *Roderick*

Random, the battle descriptions, and the accounts of military strategy have the convincing ring of authenticity, and link the Carthagena episodes of the novel very closely to the memoirs of public careers. In fact, throughout these pages Smollett almost duplicates the formula of Defoe, allowing for changes in literary fashion. Roderick himself, by his direct association with such great events and by virtue of his privileged role as their chronicler, inevitably proclaims the public importance of his own life. In a quite spectacular way, his performance in giving his account of the Carthagena affair merges the functions of biographer and historian. Smollett's hero thus demonstrates dramatically how nearly inseparable the two functions could sometimes be in this period. In an extremely explicit manner that neither Richardson nor Fielding ever quite attempted, Roderick's story also reveals how very intimately the two dimensions of private and public life were thought to touch upon one another. Viewed in this light, the Carthegena chapters of *Roderick Random* appear to be a deliberate as well as complete paradigm of the most crucial interests cultivated by all the contemporary kinds of pseudobiographical and pseudohistorical stories. To say the least, Smollett made capital use of what he knew about these minor but important works of narrative literature as he readied his own first novel for the press.

The numerous and varied works of pseudohistory and feigned historical biography were, as I have already suggested, deliberate responses to public tastes. In a kind of circular process familiar enough to anyone who has studied literary history at all, by catering to those tastes with such energy and enthusiasm writers inevitably helped to reinforce them, actually deepening the yearnings of their audience for more of the same. Apparently, contemporary readers could never get enough of stories offering a fantasy life which exalted private experience, gave it public visibility, and emphatically affirmed its importance. Certainly that is the lesson of the popularity earned by the kinds of narrative studied in this chapter, and the same general appeal, though in different manifestations, characterizes the more strictly biographical accounts of social outcasts and pious heroes and heroines to be discussed in the next two chapters. It also, of course, was the chief appeal of the new form of the novel as it emerged in the 1740s. If authors had not tried to satisfy popular tastes—an almost unimaginable possibility given the general opportunism of the writing and publishing businesses in the period—then presumably the novel as we know it would have had to await a later birth. Popular stories in historical and biographical modes were rarely the acknowledged products of the imagination, but by sheer repetition they familiarized their readers with important conventions and a kind of subject matter to which novelists like Richardson, Fielding, and Smollett found it easy to turn when composing their own more able and ambitious works.

It is not necessary to argue the degree to which these three major novelists may have copied this or that convention from this or that type of popular history or biography. What they do borrow they adapt or transform, usually quite radically, making it their own. Sometimes their borrowing is very direct, most often it is not so direct, and occasionally (as in the case of the naval chapters of *Roderick Random*) one of their works will combine the attractions of several kinds of narrative in a single episode, a concentrated series of related scenes, and so forth. Nor would it be useful to debate the broader question of whether the ingenious eclecticism of the major novelists was in every instance of its complexity a calculated response to, or borrowing from, some mode of pseudobiography, or pseudohistory, or (for that matter) romance or novelistic narrative. In the present connection at least, it is much more meaningful simply to observe that the biographical histories of Richardson, Fielding, and Smollett were written in a context which included many other lesser works that made something like the same general appeal even while disguising themselves (however transparently) as true stories of real people. The currency of these forgotten tales, we may say, despite their inferior literary quality, very likely helped encourage the chroniclers of the lives and times of Pamela Andrews, Tom Jones, and Roderick Random to write in the manner they all three adopted.

Chronology

1721   Tobias Smollett baptized in Cardross, Dumbartonshire, Scotland. He is the third child of Archibald and Barbara Smollett, whose marriage had alienated Archibald's father. Archibald dies soon after Smollett's birth, leaving family without income, probably dependent on a cousin.

ca. 1727   Enters Dumbarton Grammar School.

1735   Begins work at a Glasgow dispensary; perhaps studies medicine at Glasgow University. Writes satires.

1736   Apprenticed to two Glasgow surgeons but released in 1739 because of a cough.

1739   Arrives in London, bringing the manuscript of *The Regicide,* a tragedy, which he tries unsuccessfully to have produced for eight years.

1740   Passes examination for naval service. Receives his warrant as surgeon's second mate. Probably begins service on the *Chichester*'s expedition to Cartagena.

1741–44   Activities uncertain: perhaps stays in the navy; lives in Jamaica for some time. Marries Anne Lassells, heiress of a Jamaican plantation owner.

1744–45   Practices as a surgeon in London. First publication, *A New Song,* set to music by James Oswald (later reprinted in revised form in *Roderick Random*).

1746   Writes *The Tears of Scotland,* a poem on the atrocities of the Duke of Cumberland's troops at the Battle of Culloden. Publishes *Advice,* a verse satire.

1747   *Reproof,* sequel to *Advice,* published. His only child, Elizabeth, is born this year or the next.

1748   Publication of *The Adventures of Roderick Random* and a translation of Lesage's *Gil Blas.*

1749   *The Regicide* finally published. Visits Flanders, Holland, and France. His *Alceste,* a tragic opera and masque, is not produced, nor is his comedy *The Absent Man.*

1750   Receives medical degree from Marischal College, Aberdeen. Travels to Paris in the summer.

1751   Publishes *The Adventures of Peregrine Pickle* and three reviews in Griffiths's *Monthly Review*: John Cleland's *Memoirs of a Coxcomb,* Dr. William Smellie's *Treatise on the Theory and Practice of Midwifery,* and Dr. John Pringle's *Observations on the Diseases of the Army.*

1752   Publishes his *Essay on the External Use of Water,* exposing unhygienic conditions at Bath and defending a surgeon under attack for having taken a similar stand. An attack on Fielding, *A Faithful Narrative . . . of Habbakkuk Hilding,* attributed to Smollett.

1753   Publishes *Adventures of Ferdinand Count Fathom.* Tried in the King's Bench for assault on Peter Gordon, who had refused to repay a loan, and Gordon's landlord; Smollett is forced to pay damages and costs. Visits Scotland. Increased signs of an asthmatic condition.

1754   Publishes his edition of Alexander Drummond's travel book, *Travels through Different Cities of Germany, Italy, Greece, and Several Parts of Asia.* Translates from French *Select Essays on Commerce.* Edits the second volume of Dr. Smellie's *Cases in Midwifery.* Makes proposals in the *Public Advertiser* for a translation of *Don Quixote.*

1755   His translation of *Don Quixote,* begun in 1748, published.

1756   Begins publishing the *Critical Review,* which he edits until 1763. He is the general editor of a seven-volume anthology, *A Compendium of Authentic and Entertaining Voyages,* which comes out in April.

1757   Publishes the first three volumes of his *Complete History of England*. His farce *The Reprisal; or the Tars of Old England* is produced and published.

1758   Publishes revised edition of *Peregrine Pickle,* omitting the attacks on Garrick and some others. Fourth volume and complete revision of the *Complete History* published. His review of Admiral Charles Knowles's defense of his conduct as Rochefort leads to a suit for libel; to save the publisher, Smollett acknowledges authorship. Travels to the Continent for his health.

1759–65   Is one of the editors of *The Modern Part of the Universal History.*

1760   Together with Goldsmith, starts publishing the *British Magazine, or Monthly Repository;* remains as coeditor until 1763. Begins the weekly publication of parts of the *Continuation of the Complete History of England.* Serializes *The Adventures of Sir Launcelot Greaves* in the *British Magazine;* this is the first serialization of work by an important novelist. Probably visits Scotland. Jailed in the King's Bench Prison for libel of Admiral Knowles.

1761   Released from prison, probably before the three-month sentence is completed. Publishes the first volume of *The Works of . . . Voltaire,* an eight-year project of which he is coeditor.

1762   *Sir Launcelot Greaves* appears in book form. Begins publishing *The Briton* in support of Lord Bute. His mother-in-law dies, leaving an inheritance to his wife.

1763   Daughter Elizabeth dies. Travels to France and Italy.

1765   Returns to London; travels for health to Bath and Hot Wells. Publishes fifth and final volume of the *Continuation of the Complete History of England.*

1766   Publishes *Travels through France and Italy.* In poor health, visits Scotland, then goes to Bath and stays until 1768.

1767   For the third time rejected for a consulship.

1768   Goes to Pisa.

1769   Publication of *The Present State of All Nations,* in eight volumes, and *The History and Adventures of an Atom,* presumably his. Settles in Antignano, near Leghorn.

1771   Publishes *The Expedition of Humphry Clinker.* Dies of acute intestinal infection; buried in the English cemetery at Leghorn.

1773   *Ode to Independence* published posthumously.

1776   His translation of Fénélon's *Adventures of Telemachus* published.

Contributors

HAROLD BLOOM, Sterling Professor of the Humanities at Yale University, is the author of *The Anxiety of Influence, Poetry and Repression,* and many other volumes of literary criticism. His forthcoming study, *Freud: Transference and Authority,* attempts a full-scale reading of all of Freud's major writings. A MacArthur Prize Fellow, he is general editor of five series of literary criticism published by Chelsea House. During 1987–88, he was appointed Charles Eliot Norton Professor of Poetry at Harvard University.

RONALD PAULSON is Professor of English at The Johns Hopkins University. His books include *Popular and Polite Art in the Age of Hogarth and Fielding, Literary Landscape: Turner and Constable, Book and Painting: Shakespeare, Milton, and the Bible,* and *Representations of Revolution.*

ROBERT HOPKINS is Professor of English at the University of California at Davis. Besides numerous articles on eighteenth-century literature, he has written *The True Genius of Oliver Goldsmith.*

T. O. TREADWELL is Lecturer in English at the Roehampton Institute of Higher Education.

PHILIP STEVICK is Professor of English at Temple University. His books include *Alternative Pleasures: Postrealist Fiction and the Tradition, Anti-Story: An Anthology of Experimental Fiction,* and *The Chapter in Fiction: Theories of Narrative Division.*

THOMAS R. PRESTON is Professor of English at the University of Wyoming. He is the author of *Not in Timon's Manner: Feeling, Misanthropy, and Satire in Eighteenth-Century England.*

MICHAEL ROSENBLUM is a member of the Department of English at Indiana University.

PAUL-GABRIEL BOUCÉ teaches at the Sorbonne, where he is Professor of eighteenth-century English literature. He has published extensively on Smollett and the eighteenth-century novel and is editor-in-chief of *Études Anglaises*.

DAMIAN GRANT is a lecturer in English literature at Manchester University. Besides his study of Smollett's style, he has written poems and articles on modern poetry in various journals.

JERRY C. BEASLEY is Professor of English at the University of Delaware and the author of, among other works, *Novels of the 1740s*.

Bibliography

Batten, Charles, Jr. "*Humphry Clinker* and Eighteenth-Century Travel Literature." *Genre* 7 (1974): 392–408.

Beasley, Jerry C. "Smollett's Novels: *Ferdinand Count Fathom* for the Defense." *Papers on Language and Literature* 20 (1984): 165–84.

———. *Novels of the 1740s.* Athens: University of Georgia Press, 1982.

Bloch, Tuvia. "Smollett's Quest for Form." *Modern Philology* 65 (1967): 103–13.

Bold, Alan, ed. *Smollett: Author of the First Distinction.* London: Vision, 1982.

Boucé, Paul-Gabriel. *The Novels of Tobias Smollett.* London and New York: Longman, 1976.

———. " 'Snakes in Iceland': The 'Picaresque' in Smollett's *Roderick Random* (1748)." *Caliban* 22 (1983): 29–39.

Bourgeois, Susan. "The Domestication of the Launcelot Legend in Smollett's *Sir Launcelot Greaves.*" *Publications of the Missouri Philological Association* 8 (1983): 45–50.

Bunn, James. "Signs of Randomness in *Roderick Random.*" *Eighteenth-Century Studies* 14 (1981): 452–69.

Campbell Ross, Ian. "Language, Structure, and Vision in Smollett's *Roderick Random.*" *Études Anglaises* 31, no. 1 (1978): 52–63.

Day, Robert Adams. "Sex, Scatology, Smollett." In *Sexuality in Eighteenth-Century Britain,* edited by Paul-Gabriel Boucé. Manchester: Manchester University Press, 1982.

———. "*Ut Pictura Poesis:* Smollett, Satire, and the Graphic Arts." *Studies in Eighteenth-Century Culture* 10 (1981): 297–312.

Evans, David. "*Humphry Clinker:* Smollett's Tempered Augustanism." *Criticism* 9 (1967): 257–74.

Folkenflik, Robert. "Self and Society: Comic Union in *Humphry Clinker.*" *Philological Quarterly* 53 (1974): 195–204.

Grant, Damian. *Tobias Smollett: A Study in Style.* Manchester: Manchester University Press, 1977.

Iser, Wolfgang. *The Implied Reader: Patterns of Communication in Prose Fiction from Bunyan to Beckett.* Baltimore: Johns Hopkins University Press, 1974.

Kahrl, George L. "The Influence of Shakespeare on Smollett." In *Essays in Dramatic Literature: The Parrott Presentation Volume,* 399–420. Princeton: Princeton University Press, 1935.

Knapp, Lewis. *Tobias Smollett: Doctor of Men and Manners*. Princeton: Princeton University Press, 1949.

Miles, Peter. "A Semi-Mental Journey: Structure and Illusion in Smollett's *Travels*." *Prose Studies 5*, no. 1 (1982): 43–60.

———. "Platonic Topography and the Locations of *Humphry Clinker*." *Trivium* 16 (May 1981): 81–98.

New, Melvyn. " 'The Grease of God': The Form of Eighteenth-Century English Fiction." *PMLA* 91 (1976): 235–44.

Orwell, George. "Smollett." In *Collected Essays, Journalism, and Letters III*. Harmondsworth: Penguin, 1970.

Park, William. "Fathers and Sons—*Humphry Clinker*." *Literature and Psychology* 16, nos. 3 and 4 (1966): 166–74.

Paulson, Ronald. *Satire and the Novel in Eighteenth-Century England*. New Haven: Yale University Press, 1967.

———. "Satire in the Early Novels of Smollett." *Journal of English and Germanic Philology* 59 (1960): 381–402.

Preston, Thomas. "Smollett and the Benevolent Misanthrope Type." *PMLA* 79 (1964): 51–57.

———. "Disenchanting the Man of Feeling: Smollett's *Ferdinand Count Fathom*." In *Quick Springs of Sense: Studies in the Eighteenth Century,* edited by Larry S. Champion. Athens: University of Georgia Press, 1974.

Price, John Vladimir. *Tobias Smollett: The Expedition of* Humphry Clinker. London: Edward Arnold, 1973.

Pritchett, V. S. *The Living Novel*. New York: Random House, 1964.

Punter, David. "Smollett and the Logic of Domination." *Literature and History* 1 (1975): 60–83.

Reid, B. L. "Smollett's Healing Journey." *The Virginia Quarterly Review* 41 (1965): 549–70.

Rogers, Pat. *The Augustan Vision*. New York: Barnes & Noble, 1974.

Ross, Angus. "The Show of Violence in Smollett's Novels." *Yearbook of English Studies* 77 (1972): 118–29.

Rothstein, Eric. "Scotophilia and *Humphry Clinker*: The Politics of Beggary, Bugs, and Buttocks." *University of Toronto Quarterly* 52, no. 2 (1982): 63–78.

Rousseau, G. S. *Tobias Smollett: Essays of Two Decades*. Edinburgh: T. & T. Clark, 1982.

Rousseau, G. S., and P.-G. Boucé, eds. *Tobias Smollett: Bicentennial Essays Presented to Lewis M. Knapp*. New York: Oxford University Press, 1971.

Sekora, John. *Luxury: The Concept in Western Thought, Eden to Smollett*. Baltimore and London: Johns Hopkins University Press, 1977.

Spector, Robert Donald. *Tobias George Smollett*. New York: Twayne, 1968.

Stevick, Philip. "Stylistic Energy in the Early Smollett." *Studies in Philology* 64 (1967): 712–19.

Strauss, Albrecht P. "On Smollett's Language: A Paragraph in *Ferdinand Count Fathom*." In *Style in Prose Fiction: English Institute Essays 1958*, edited by Harold C. Martin. New York: Columbia University Press, 1959.

Warner, John. "The Interpolated Narrations in the Fiction of Fielding and Smollett: An Epistemological View." *Studies in the Novel* 5 (1973): 271–83.

Acknowledgments

"Satire and Melodrama" by Ronald Paulson from *Satire and the Novel in Eighteenth-Century England* by Ronald Paulson, © 1967 by Yale University. Reprinted by permission of Yale University Press.

"The Function of Grotesque in *Humphry Clinker*" by Robert Hopkins from *Huntington Library Quarterly* 32, no. 2 (February 1969), © 1969 by *Huntington Library Quarterly*. Reprinted by permission.

"The Two Worlds of *Ferdinand Count Fathom*" by T. O. Treadwell from *Tobias Smollett: Bicentennial Essays Presented to Lewis M. Knapp*, edited by G. S. Rousseau and P.-G. Boucé, © 1971 by Oxford University Press. Reprinted by permission.

"Smollett's Picaresque Games" by Philip Stevick from *Tobias Smollett: Bicentennial Essays Presented to Lewis M. Knapp*, edited by G. S. Rousseau and P.-G. Boucé, © 1971 by Oxford University Press. Reprinted by permission.

"The 'Stage Passions' and Smollett's Characterization" by Thomas R. Preston from *Studies in Philology* 71, no. 1 (January 1974), © 1974 by the University of North Carolina Press. Reprinted by permission of the author and the University of North Carolina Press. The notes have been omitted.

"Smollett and the Old Conventions" by Michael Rosenblum from *Philological Quarterly* 55, no. 3 (Summer 1976), © 1976 by the University of Iowa. Reprinted by permission of the author and the University of Iowa.

"The Representation of the Real" by Paul-Gabriel Boucé from *The Novels of Tobias Smollett* by Paul-Gabriel Boucé, © 1976 by Librairie Marcel Didier. Reprinted by permission.

"Style at the Circumference" by Damian Grant from *Tobias Smollett: A Study in Style* by Damian Grant, © 1977 by Damian Grant. Reprinted by permission of Manchester University Press.

"Richardson, Fielding, and Smollett: Private Experience as Public History" by Jerry C. Beasley from *Novels of the 1740s* by Jerry C. Beasley, © 1982 by the University of Georgia Press. Reprinted by permission of the University of Georgia Press.

Index